W9-ABW-840

Combat Uniforms of the Civil War

A Council of War in 1861.
From left to right: Abraham
Lincoln, W. Seward, Winfield
Scott, Simon Cameron,
General McLellan, B. Butler,
J. Wool, R. Anderson,
J. Fremont and J. Dix.

Combat Uniforms of the Civil War

Volume One
The Federal Army

Mark Lloyd
Illustrated by Mike Codd

Chelsea House Publishers
Philadelphia

Published in 1999 by
Chelsea House Publishers
1974 Sproul Road, Suite 400
P.O. Box 914
Broomall, PA19008-0914

Printed in China

Library of Congress Cataloging-in-Publication Data

Lloyd, Mark 1948-
        Combat uniforms of the Civil War / Mark Lloyd:
Illustrated by Mike Codd.
        p. cm.
        Includes index.
        Summary: Describes the military uniforms worn by
individual units of Federal and Confederate armies during the
Civil War as well as the battlefield activities of these units.
        1. United States. Army—Uniforms—Juvenile literature.
2. Confederate States of America. Army—Uniforms—
Juvenile literature. 3. United States—History—Civil War,
1861-1865—Juvenile literature. [1. Military uniforms. 2.
United States. Army. 3. Confederate States of America. Army.
4. United States—History—Civil War, 1861-1865.] I. Codd,
Michael, ill. II. Title.
UC483.L55   1998
355. 1'4'0973—dc21   98-18187
                                          CIP
                                          AC

        ISBN 0-7910-4993-0 (vol. 1)
        ISBN 0-7910-4994-9 (vol. 2)
        ISBN 0-7910-4995-7 (vol. 3)
        ISBN 0-7910-4996-5 (vol. 4)
        ISBN 0-7910-4992-2 (set)

Contents

Headquarters – Army of the Potomac. General Grant and his staff, taken at City Point, 1864.

INTRODUCTION

The conflict between the American states introduced the world to the awful realities of total warfare. In four years of bitter fighting over 160,000 soldiers died in action – an estimated 90,000 of their wounds, 60,000 in prison camps and perhaps 10,000 in accidents. In many instances, details of Confederate casualties simply do not exist.

The Civil War had little to do with slavery. By 1861 the United States was one of only three nations within the American continent to tolerate the institution and all but the most reactionary conceded that its days were numbered.

During the 1850s the North and South had grown steadily apart until, by the end of that decade, a national identity had virtually ceased to exist. Huge numbers of European immigrants had flooded into the north-eastern seaboard in seach of a new life. A few had prospered but most, having found the harsh realities of crowded urban life not to their liking, had either moved west in search of space or had formed introverted ghettos. Eager to exploit the wealth of new labor, and spurred on by the advent of the industrial revolution, the inhabitants of cities such as New York, Boston and Philadelphia had transformed them into vast industrial complexes.

In complete contrast, life in the South had remained largely unchanged. Almost totally dependent on the growth and export of cotton, still feudal in its social outlook and uncompromisingly conservative, it had come to regard itself as the poor relation of the North from which it felt itself increasingly alienated. By 1861, in social and economic reality if not in political theory, the United States existed as two totally independent entities.

In hindsight, the election of Abraham Lincoln as President made war inevitable. Nevertheless when open hostilities actually began, neither side was in any way prepared for the rigors ahead. The North had made no real attempt to mobilize while the South, despite its military ancestry, had no standing army.

Patriotic men in both camps rallied to the colors only to find their national administrations sadly wanting. Frustrated, they turned to their states, to their counties, even to their townships, indeed to any viable organization attempting to form bodies of men for the war. Independent companies and battalions were formed, clothed and armed by local dignitaries rich and influential enough to do so.

Dress regulations, where they existed, were largely ignored. Volunteer units of both sides frequently dressed themselves in elaborate and quite impractical costumes more suited to the European parade ground than to war. Gradually the armies became more unkept and dishevelled as the realities of modern combat became apparent. Gaudily clad *chasseurs* and Zouaves abandoned their bright crimsons and blues in favor of the anonymity of blue or gray. Cumbersome and heavy equipment was modified for comfort and surplus issue simply discarded without a thought to the future. Issue greatcoats were abandoned in the hot summer of 1861 by raw recruits who had no concept of the pri-

vations of a winter campaign.

Of the regulation equipment, only the haversack remained universally popular. Items which would not fit into the haversack were carried rolled in a blanket over one shoulder. Few troops carried spare clothing or washing equipment. Basic sanitation was ignored, with the result that disease became rampant. Even weapons were not spared. Whole battalions, particularly within the Confederacy, abandoned their heavy and awkward bayonets to their obvious disadvantage in subsequent close quarter battle.

As the war progressed soldiers relied heavily upon their families for resupply, with the result that uniforms became increasingly civilianized. Long overcoats, colored waistcoats and all manner of individual headgear became popular. Certain general staff officers at times achieved an almost comical appearance, although there is no evidence to suggest that their attire ever detracted from their (usually) excellent military judgment. Other generals, particularly George Custer – whose ego was later destined to prove his downfall – appeared in ornate uniforms made ludicrous by quantities of gold braid and ornament.

As the Northern blockade began to bite, Confederate resupply became critical. In flagrant breach of the rules of war, clothing was looted from prisoners, many of whom subsequently died of exposure, and corpses were robbed of anything serviceable. Troops began to appear in a mishmash of issue gray and looted blue which inevitably led to confusion and a Federal threat to shoot as spies all prisoners thus clad.

To compound the problem most uniforms were made of "shoddy," an inferior substance compris-

Recruiting posters such as this helped to swell the numbers volunteering for the Union Army. The $10 bounty would have been paid from State, rather than federal, resources.

6

ing reclaimed wool and scraps, prone to disintegration under heavy treatment or in bad weather. Dyes were rarely if ever universal, particularly in the South where issue uniform varied in hue from Confederate gray to light brown. As the war progressed, "butternut," a buff dye made from boiled nutshells and iron oxide filings, predominated.

Shoes and boots were scarce from the outset and by the end of the war hardly merited such a description. Most infantrymen's shoes consisted of green untreated leather crudely nailed to a wooden sole and rarely lasted a campaign. Thereafter the unfortunate soldier was expected to make do and mend. Often this consisted of his obtaining raw hide from the regimental slaughterman, wrapping his feet in old rags and sewing the hide around them.

Extraordinarily, despite the many privations, morale remained high in many units even during the final stages of the war when soldiers traditionally look to the future and are therefore less likely to take risks.

The Civil War produced insurmountable administrative problems. It also produced some of the finest generals in American military history. Without men of the caliber of Lee, Jackson and Stuart, the South would not have survived its first winter. On the other hand, were it not for commanders of the worth of Grant, Sherman and McClellan the North could not have hoped to have fielded and controlled the massive armies which eventually overwhelmed the Confederacy and restored the Union.

It must never be forgotten that the Civil War was

fought over vast areas on a previously unknown scale. If the uniforms of 1861 seem ridiculous and the administration lacking, this is surely understandable. It was not, after all, until the First Battle of Bull Run (Manassas) that either adversary had any clear idea of the consequences of modern war. The soldiers who faced each other at Appomattox had little if anything in common with the idealists who had rushed to the enlistment offices only four short years earlier.

For the South, independence was more a matter of theory rather than fact. Within months of the secession the Confederate States had formed a union as rigid and uncompromising as that which they had left.

Bands were formed by many battalions to play their men into battle. In reality, by early 1862 most bands had been scrapped, the musicians having been transferred to less glamorous duties as medical orderlies and stretcher bearers.

THE FEDERAL ARMY

The American Civil War was the last romantic war. During the previous 50 years, Federal troops had fought first the British, then the Indians and finally the Mexicans in a series of successful, if limited, engagements. Losses had been light, the civilian population had suffered minimal inconvenience, and commerce had positively gained. Consequently, as the North/South divide grew and with it the possibility of secession and war, no one thought that the resulting hostilities would last for more than a few weeks. Absolute war was simply beyond the comprehension of all but the greatest pessimist.

The first violent act – the bombardment of Fort Sumter – had a dramatic effect on the population of the North. In the northeastern seaboard states, tens of thousands of newly arrived immigrants saw military service as a way of establishing their right to equality of treatment in a postwar society. Although many of them had lived in the United States for only a few months and were not even citizens, they demanded the right to fight for the Union. When an unprepared Federal government failed to provide them with uniforms and equipment, they turned to the states and when state resources proved inadequate, they simply formed their own companies. Many volunteered for just 90 days in the belief that the war would be fought and won in that time; only later did the states call for two-year volunteers. Units which formed locally naturally looked to their own society for leadership. Officers were elected by their own men on the basis of their social standing without reference to their military potential. Colonels with little or no formal training led their fledgling regiments into battle, and, on occasion, into wholesale destruction.

Ethnic minorities which had been forced by religious and/or social differences to live in overcrowded, unsanitary ghettos formed regiments from within their own communities. For example, the Irish Brigade was formed exclusively from New York, Boston and Philadelphia immigrants by Thomas Francis Meagher, an influential first-generation American who had been banished by the British to Tasmania for sedition and treasonous activity, only to escape to the United States in 1852.

The 79th New York (Highlanders) were formed from Scottish immigrants, many of whom had seen service with the British army during the Crimean War. Dour, hardy and deeply religious, they encompassed completely the traditions and discipline of a European regular army. Even when they were expanded to ten companies with the introduction of Irish and English expatriates, they refused to compromise their heritage, continuing to parade in the full dress uniform of the 79th (Cameron Highlanders) from whom they took their traditions.

Where traditions did not exist, they were often invented. Troops who had little idea where North Africa was eagerly donned the gaudy uniform of the French colonial Zouave regiments. Others wore less dramatic but, as history was to prove, far more realistic gray or blue.

The 1st Battle of Manassas (Bull Run) brought home to the North the full realities and horror of war. On 16 July 1861 the Union army moved south from Washington to march against the Confederates. No formal battle plan existed nor were the troops provisioned adequately for the hot days ahead. The 30-mile march to Manassas Junction took two full days, during which good order and military discipline largely disintegrated. The troops were further impeded by the presence of a large number of civilians who had driven out from Washington to watch their heroes annihilate the enemy. In terms of ground captured, the battle itself was indecisive. The Confederates held the field, forcing the green Union troops to retreat in total disorder toward the safety of Washington, but they failed completely to consolidate their victory. The losses were, however, staggering: of the 35,000 Union troops committed to battle (many of whom were held in reserve and actually saw no action), 460 were killed, 1,124 wounded and 1,312 captured or reported missing. At once the harsh realities of war became apparent. Wholly inappropriate European-orientated dress uniforms were abandoned in favor of plain serge. Gray uniforms were dyed blue lest the wearers be mistaken for the enemy, as had happened at Manassas. Two-year volunteers replaced 90-day men, and ultimately conscription was introduced. By 1863 the Union felt confident enough to take the initiative and introduced a policy of total war never before seen on the American continent.

As the conflict grew in momentum and ferocity, supply outstripped demand, forcing the Union to purchase arms and equipment from every source available. Gradually the rifled musket, mostly imported from Europe, began to replace the smoothbore until, by 1865, the latter was a rarity. Early artillery, much of which had seen action in the Mexican wars, was replaced by far superior Napoleons and occasionally by rifled muzzle-loaders with their greater range and accuracy. Massed Union artillery reasserted itself as the true "God of War." Specialist units – medics, engineers, signalers, supply and ordnance, each with their own distinctive uniforms and insignia – began to play an important part in the order of battle.

By 1865, the Union army was a hardened, thoroughly professional force. Its commanders, once sadly lacking in expertise, were now second to none. In keeping with an army trained to live off the (enemy) land, its troops had learned to travel light whenever possible to facilitate speed and maneuverability and were capable of covering considerable distances without additional support. Federal cavalry, once the Cinderella of the battlefield, had learned from its mistakes and, at Brandy Station, had actually checked the seemingly invincible Confederates. Few armies in history have grown as fast and as positively as the Union forces between 1861 and 1865.

ULYSSES S. GRANT

Few military leaders have ever shown less early promise than Ulysses S. Grant. Born the son of an Ohio tanner on 27 April 1822, Grant was originally named Hiram Ulysses but decided to reverse his names when enrolling for West Point in 1839. Inexplicably the registration was erroniously made in the name of "Ulysses S. Grant," a name which he eventually accepted, maintaining to the end that the "S" did not stand for anything. Never a natural soldier, there is evidence to suggest that Grant agreed to attend West Point simply as a means of continuing his education and that he had no intention whatsoever of making a formal career of the army. Graduating 21st in a class of 39, Grant distinguished himself in horsemanship and showed considerable promise in mathematics, neither of which he was able to exploit fully in his first few years with the colors. Assigned as brevet second lieutenant to the 4th U.S. Infantry upon graduation in 1843, he was posted to St. Louis, Missouri where he met and, in 1848, married Julia Boggs Dent, by whom he eventually had four children.

The young soldier's first taste of battle came with the Mexican War of 1846–48 during which he received two citations for gallantry and one for meritorious conduct while serving under General Zachary Taylor. Promoted to the rank of brevet captain in recognition of his bravery, he however remained a substantive first lieutenant reverting to that rank after the war until his formal promotion in August 1853.

On 5 July 1852, when the 4th Infantry sailed from New York to undertake a tour of duty at Fort Vancouver in Oregon Territory on the west coast, Grant left his family behind rather than submit them to the dangers of the Isthmus of Panama. Impoverished, lonely for his family, and increasingly unable to bear the futility and monotony of postwar military service, Grant began drinking heavily and neglecting his duty. Determined to be reunited with his family, he entered into a number of unsuccessful business ventures in an attempt to raise capital, but only compounded his misfortune. Promoted to captain and posted to Fort Humboldt, California in 1853, Grant's lifestyle immediately brought him into conflict with an unsympathetic commanding officer, as a result of which he chose voluntary resignation the following year rather than face the possibility of court martial, which could well have gone against him.

During the next few years, Grant became increasingly destitute as he failed at a number of undertakings. Attempts to eke out an existence by farming 80 acres given to his wife Julia by her father proved less than successful, as did a speculative partnership in the volatile world of realty.

On the outbreak of the Civil War, a thankful and by now thoroughly frustrated Grant offered his services unreservedly to the Union. He helped recruit, equip, and drill troops in the Galena area of northwest Illinois before accompanying them to the state capital at Springfield, where Governor Richard Yates appointed him an aide and assigned him to the state adjutant general's office. Promoted

General Ulysses S. Grant in typical pose, photographed at City Point, Virginia, in August 1864.

colonel by the governor in June 1861 and given command of the 21st Illinois Volunteers, a somewhat unruly unit then in formation, Grant was almost immediately elevated to brigadier general at the instigation of Congressman Elihu Washburne, and was given control of the District of Southeast Missouri based on Cairo at the southernmost tip of Illinois, where the Ohio and Mississippi rivers meet.

Frustrated by the inactivity that marked the first few months of the war in the West, Grant allowed his impatience to get the better of him when he was ordered to make a limited demonstration of power along the banks of the Mississippi. Acting on his own, and in the mistaken belief that a sizeable Confederate raiding party was about to move into Missouri, Grant led a mixed force of 3,114 infantry and cavalry supported by a battery of six guns in a formal assault against the Confederate position at Belmont. Although the attack was successful, Grant was nearly cut off from his own lines and forced to retire amid some confusion. The Federals lost a total of 607 men compared with Southern casualties of 642, and Grant learned a valuable lesson about overcommitment.

In 1862, Grant at last received permission to go onto the offensive and, on 16 February, won the Union its first major victory when, in Tennessee, he forced the surrender of Fort Donelson with its garrison of 15,000 troops. Promotion to major general followed, as did national acclaim. However, the gratitude of a civilian population toward the military has always been notoriously fickle, and veneration turned to hostility in April of that year when Grant's troops sustained 1,754 killed while driving off an unexpected Confederate attack at Shiloh Church. Grant was relieved of command, which reverted to General Halleck. When the latter was recalled to Washington as general-in-chief of the army in July 1862, Grant was restored to his command – a position which, in hindsight, he should never have lost.

In the latter part of 1862, Grant began his advance toward Vicksburg, the last major Confederate stronghold on the Mississippi and one of the strongest natural defensive positions in the country. Grant's natural drive, aggressiveness, and perception of tactics did much to accelerate the fall of the city, which surrendered, aptly enough, on 4 July 1863. When Port Hudson, Louisiana fell a few days later, the entire Mississippi passed under Federal control, effectively bisecting the Confederacy.

After his subsequent victory at Chattanooga, Grant was promoted to lieutenant general (9 March 1864) and, three days later, was appointed "General-in-Chief of the Armies of the United States." He at once took over the strategic direction of the war and set about the economic and military destruction of the South. Utilizing fully the numerically vastly superior forces at his disposal, he ordered General Meade with the Army of the Potomac to continue its relentless war of attrition against Robert E. Lee's Army of Northern Virginia, while General Sherman cut a swathe of destruction through Georgia.

Grant's strongest points at this time – his drive, his versatility, and his receptiveness to innovation – were also, ironically, often his greatest enemies. Never a man to court fools nor to waste time on the niceties of etiquette, he would frequently pass direct orders to regiments in action, ignoring completely the usual chain of command. On more than one occasion, the long-suffering General Meade found his orders countermanded or his troops committed to a course of action of which he knew nothing. Had it not been for the extreme professionalism of his staff, it is more than likely that Grant's well-meaning but precipitant actions would have led to chaos.

In late 1865, within a few months of engineering its defeat, Grant toured the South at the request of President Andrew Johnson and was given so friendly a reception that he submitted a report advocating leniency. In 1866, he was appointed to the newly created rank of "General of the Armies" and a year later accepted the appointment of Secretary of War. His appointment was, however, blatantly political, and when Congress demanded the reinstatement of his predecessor Edwin Stanton, he resigned to the considerable chagrin of Johnson who felt that Grant had let him down.

Grant was nominated as Republican candidate for the presidency in 1868 and, on 4 March 1869, entered the White House. Politically inexperienced and, at the age of 46, the youngest President thus far, Grant was honest and well meaning but too reliant on his advisers to be a success. Although returned for a second term of office, the final years of his tenure were marked by a series of scandals. The Secretary of War, William Belknap, was impeached for taking bribes, but although a majority of Senators voted to convict him, there was not the necessary two-thirds. Those who voted to acquit him did not believe in his innocence; they simply considered that they no longer had jurisdiction over Belknap because he had resigned his office.

In 1884, the still commercially naive Grant entered into a financial venture with the unscrupulous Ferdinand Ward, as a result of which he lost his entire life savings. Fortunately, however, he had signed a contract for the publication of his memoirs, which were eventually a great success with over 300,000 copies sold. In agony from cancer of the throat and scarcely able to eat, he labored on with his memoirs, determined to finish them before he died. In July 1885, a few weeks after completing his much acclaimed book, he died peacefully and now lies buried in Riverside Park, New York City.

Before his own untimely death, Lincoln described his great friend in two simple, succinct words: "He fights." Colonel Theodore Lyman of Meade's staff was more forthright, if no more accurate, when he described Grant as "rather under middle height, of a spare strong build; light-brown hair, and short, light-brown beard ... eyes of a clear blue; forehead high; nose aquiline; jaw squarely set, but not sensual. His face has three expressions: deep thought; extreme determination; and great simplicity and calmness."

Ulysses S. Grant was never a smart soldier, preferring to dress for comfort rather than dignity. His uniform coat and waistcoat were invariably unbuttoned, his black felt slouch hat often missing. Frequently he discarded his sword, spurs and sash and might easily have been mistaken for a somewhat disheveled civilian had it not been for the three gold bars of a lieutenant-general which he wore on his shoulder straps.

5TH NEW YORK VOLUNTEERS (DURYEE ZOUAVES)

Many volunteer regiments of the Union and Confederate armies modeled themselves on the dashing Zouaves of the French colonial service. The original Zouaves (pronounced zoo-aves) were Algerian light infantry troops famous for their marksmanship (particularly their ability to fire and reload from the prone position), for the precision of their drill, and, above all, for their dress. Although regiments varied, all wore bright gaudy colors, baggy trousers, short open jackets with gaiters and either a turban or fez.

Despite the relatively small influence of French culture on the pre-war North, Zouave uniforms became very popular with the many militia units formed in the late 1850's and early 1860's in response to the growing threat of political unrest in the South. Many volunteer regiments were raised by general consensus and public subscription. Others were mustered by wealthy individuals, often but by no means always with previous military experience, who then assumed the mantle of command. Abram Duryee, a highly successful New York City merchant, had been active in the state militia prior to the outbreak of the Civil War, twice sustaining wounds during the 1849 Astor Place riots. On the outbreak of hostilities, therefore, he was ideally placed to raise his own unit and, on 25 April 1861, was gazetted the first colonel of the 5th New York Volunteers (Duryee Zouaves).

The 5th New York became one of the most illustrious of all volunteer regiments, earning the esteem of the regular troops with whom it operated and the approbation of General George Sykes, the commander of V Corps, Army of the Potomac, under whom it served throughout the bloodiest stages of the war.

Initially, many inexperienced volunteer officers regarded drill, regulation dress, and such overt acts of discipline as saluting as a wasteful distraction from the fighting. However, Duryee, the one-time colonel-in-chief of the 7th New York State Militia, realized the need for strict discipline and demanded from the outset consistently high standards from his subordinates. As a direct result, the regiment gained an enviable reputation for unsurpassed smartness on parade, a factor which later manifested itself on the battlefield at Gaines's Mill (27 June 1862) when, under withering volley fire, it gained the respect of friend and foe alike by halting, "counting off," and realigning its ranks before continuing its assault.

Due to its proficiency, the regiment was given the honor of serving as part of "Sykes Regulars," a division within V Corps otherwise comprising professional soldiers. Commanded at various times by Duryee, G.K. Warren, Hiram Duryea, and Cleveland Winslow, its members fought at the battles of Big Bethel, Gaine's Mill, Manassas, Shepherdstown Ford, Fredericksburg, and Chancellorsville and at the Yorktown siege. During the final stages of the 2nd Battle of Manassas (29–30 August 1862) – also known as the 2nd Battle of Bull Run – the 5th New York Zouaves sustained 117 killed out of 490 in action, the highest losses of any infantry regiment in the war and a rate of attrition from which it never fully recovered.

Manassas began ominously for the North. Despite their vast superiority in numbers and equipment, the Union armies had failed totally to halt, let alone destroy, the superbly motivated and far more versatile Confederate forces. Command of the newly formed Army of Virginia had been delegated to John Pope, a relatively junior major general whose sole recent field experience had been gained with the Army of the Mississippi in the West. From the outset, Pope made himself unpopular with officers and men alike, compounding the problem by delivering an ill-timed and ill-conceived introductory address in which he made ample reference to the virtues of his old command to the detriment of his new. Even the enigmatic General Robert E. Lee expressed disgust at the severity of several of the marshal law edicts introduced by Pope into the occupied areas of Virginia.

Immediately upon assuming his new command, Pope used his geographical proximity to Washington advantageously, tirelessly lobbying Lincoln and General Henry Halleck, the newly appointed general-in-chief of the U.S. land forces, until both agreed to allow his army to attempt an overland assault on Richmond from the north. McClellan's Army of the Potomac, currently bogged down in the Peninsula campaign, would assume a subordinate role.

Impatient for victory, Pope moved his forces on the Confederacy on 12 July. Fully aware of the impossibility of fighting on two fronts, Lee rightly guessed that Pope and not McClellan now posed the immediate threat, and so he ordered Major General "Stonewall" Jackson with 11,000 men north to hinder his advance. Gradually Lee sent Jackson more reinforcements until, by early August, he had a corps of 24,000 under his command. On 3 August,

Fighting as part of Sykes Regular Corps, the 5th New York sustained 117 fatalities during the Second Battle of Bull Run

Headdress: Unusually, the officers dressed less ostentatiously than their men. While the latter paraded in a white turban and wore a blue-tasselled cap in the field, the officers contented themselves with a red and blue kepi.

Uniform: Whereas the rank and file were issued with a conventional Zouave-pattern jacket, shirt and pantaloons, again the officers restricted themselves to a variant of the regulation frock coat, adorned with Confederate-style cuff-braid and sash, and red trousers.

McClellan was ordered to disengage in the Peninsula and to join Pope in a concerted attack. Lee at once moved north with the 28,000 men of Longstreet's Corps, many of them Texans, in a desperate attempt to link up with Jackson and defeat Pope before the latter could be reinforced by McClellan. Everything would depend on luck and perfect timing.

Pope's advance was halted on 9 August when his leading units met elements of Jackson's Corps on Cedar Mountain. The Union forces withdrew behind the Rappahannock River to await reinforcements; the stage was set for confrontation. In an attempt to maneuver Pope from his strong position, Lee ordered Jackson to execute a left flanking movement behind the Federal lines. With his rail link thus cut and his supply lines to Washington and to Alexandria across the Potomac from the capital denied him, Lee reasoned that Pope would have to chase Jackson, allowing Lee and Longstreet to bring up the residue of the Confederate army across the Rappahannock. Pope initially dismissed Jackson's move as nothing more than a diversionary raid into the Shenandoah Valley, and it was not until elements of Confederate cavalry led by J.E.B. Stuart appeared at Manassas Junction on 26 August that he fully realized the extent of the threat to his rear.

Pope immediately ordered his army to abandon its position on the Rappahannock and to proceed to Manassas Junction, just southwest of the small river known as Bull Run. Simultaneously Jackson moved his small force north and took up a defensive position behind the banks of an unfinished railroad. Fearful that Jackson might escape him, and heedless of the whereabouts of Longstreet's Corps, which in the interim had moved fast to attempt to link up with Jackson's exhausted and hard-pressed forces, Pope ordered a full frontal assault without first establishing the exact size and disposition of the enemy. Throughout Saturday, 29 August, Jackson's troops parried attack after attack, sustaining

Colonel Abram Duryee, an experienced soldier, administrator and first commander of the 5th New York.

terrible casualties until nightfall brought a brief respite. So confident of victory was Pope that he again discounted the whereabouts of Longstreet's as yet uncommitted troops.

On Sunday, 30 August, Pope ordered a final assault on the depleted Confederate lines. The 5th New York Zouaves were deployed on the extreme left flank, the weakest part of the attack. Unknown to Pope, Longstreet's fresh corps had joined Jackson during the night and was now deployed on the Confederate right, directly opposite the hapless and unsuspecting New Yorkers. In the early afternoon, 18 Confederate guns were suddenly brought into action, tearing great swathes in the already thin lines of Federal attackers. Still the Union troops pressed forward until by 4:00 p.m. their lines

were broken. Seizing his opportunity, Lee ordered Longstreet's infantry to counter-attack. The Union left flank held briefly but eventually succumbed to the Texan onslaught. Pope was driven from the field and, but for the heroic actions of a few units, would have stood no chance of regrouping. As has already been stated, the 5th New York lost heavily during the counter-attack and indeed never fully recovered. However, had it not been for the bravery which it demonstrated during that fateful Sunday afternoon, the subsequent rout might have turned into annihilation.

Unusually for a two-year regiment, "Duryee's Zouaves" contained a number of three-year enlistees. When the Regiment's enlistment expired, therefore, many of its volunteers were transferred

into the 146th New York. Colonel Winslow subsequently reorganized the 5th New York, and sustained fatal injuries as its commander in the Battle of Bethesda Church, ten miles from Richmond, Virginia, but the new unit contained none of the panache of the old.

The 5th New York were generally considered the smartest of all the Zouave regiments in the Union army. Officers' uniforms were somewhat less ostentatious than those of their men which closely resembled the French original. For full dress, the enlisted men wore a white turban round the fez, russet leather and white canvas gaiters bound with black leather straps, voluminous red trousers and a blue *chasseur*'s jacket. In the field, the fez was replaced by a red stocking cap.

Had it not been for the bravery exhibited by the already decimated 5th New York, the retreat from Bull Run would have turned into a rout with disastrous consequences for the North.

9TH NEW YORK VOLUNTEERS (HAWKINS' ZOUAVES)

Despite months of forewarning, the Union was far from ready for war when the Confederacy eventually seceded in the spring of 1861. The majority of the 16,000 strong regular army was scattered in 79 frontier posts west of the Mississippi; 90 percent of the navy was thousands of miles away in foreign waters; and the military reserve remained firmly under jealously guarded state control. Early Federal attempts to raise 75,000 "90–day volunteers" from among the militia met with ridicule when it was realized that the war would most certainly last for more than three months and would inevitably require far more than 75,000 men to bring about victory. On 3 May 1861, Lincoln authorized the induction of a further 42,000 three-year volunteers, but by then, many of the states had seized the initiative and had enrolled their own two-year volunteers.

Frustrated by what they regarded as the lack of purpose at Federal Government level, state governors, city councils, and, occasionally, philanthropic individuals raised independent units, clothing, feeding, and where possible training the troops until Washington was able to absorb them into the Union army. Governors sent purchasing agents to Europe where they competed with each other and with their Confederate rivals for the acquisition of surplus uniforms and ammunition. New York State, for instance, acquired thousands of Zouave uniforms regardless of their impracticality and despite the fact that the majority of its citizens were Anglo-Saxon rather than French.

Volunteer regiments retained close ties with their states and municipalities. Enlisted men elected many of their officers from within the community and the governors appointed the rest. Companies and even whole regiments often consisted of men from a single township, city, or county. Although, initially, this did much to enhance morale both among the men and their relatives waiting at home, as the war progressed the effects of a single bloody battle in which losses of 50 percent were not unusual were calamitous.

Once formed, a regiment did not receive reinforcements to replace the dead and injured. Instead it simply diminished in size and effectiveness until,

A wounded Zouave of the Federal Army is guarded by a Confederate.

Headdress: Although a scarlet fez was retained for formal wear, most troops favored a soft dark red woolen cap in the field.

Jacket: A sky-blue overcoat was worn over a dark blue jacket and *chasseur*-pattern dark blue trousers. Despite the total lack of camouflage, the uniform was retained until the regiment's disbandment in 1863.

Gaiters: White gaiters, originally made of russet but later constructed of pigskin or canvas, were worn over conventional black boots.

at the end of its contractual recruitment period, it was disbanded.

The 9th New York Volunteers exemplify perfectly the early two-year state-organized regiment. Its members were primarily drawn from Albany, Brooklyn, Hyde Park, Mount Vernon, Staten Island, and parts of Connecticut and New Jersey, supplemented by a few friends and relatives from as far afield as Canada. The majority of the officers were American born, and a few possessed considerable previous military experience. The lieutenant colonel, George F. Belts, although a lawyer by profession, had been a militia field officer. Major Edgar Kimball had been breveted for gallantry at Chirubusco and Contreras as a captain while serving with the 9th U.S. Infantry in 1847/48 during the Mexican War, and the regimental surgeon had seen active service with both the British and the French.

If the regiment was conventional, its commander was most definitely not. Born in 1831, Rush Christopher Hawkins served as a junior officer in the Mexican War while still a minor. Anticipating secession with all its ramifications, Hawkins formed a military club in 1860 with himself as president, and a year later, on 4 May 1861, he transformed it into a fighting unit. He then offered it, with himself at its head, to the state of New York.

Hawkins subsequently married Annmary Brown, the daughter of the founder of Brown University, Rhode Island, and after making a fortune from real estate and investments, he dedicated the last years of his life to the collection of rare 15th-century books. At the time of his death in 1920, Hawkins was reputed to have had a collection second only to that of the British Museum.

The Regiment – which inevitably became known as "Hawkins' Zouaves" after its charismatic leader and mode of dress – fought as part of the Army of the Potomac in the Maryland campaign, on South Mountain, at Antietam (Sharpsburg), and in eastern Virginia, before being mustered out on 20 May 1863, having lost 358 officers and men on active service.

The Union armies of 1862 were poorly led, and after the 1st Battle of Manassas/Bull Run (in which the 9th New York played no part), they were demoralized. When Lee crossed the Potomac on 5 September 1862, entered Maryland, and invaded the North, McClellan, commanding the Army of the Potomac, failed to take decisive action. Instead he allowed the Confederates to divide their forces and advance simultaneously on Harpers Ferry and Sharpsburg. Despite ample evidence of Lee's intentions, set out fully in a captured copy of his field

Recruiting for Hawkins' New York Zouaves. The recruiting drive attracted a large body of men to its ranks, nearly all of them under 30 years of age.

orders, McClellan insisted in pursuing the enemy to Sharpsburg, leaving Harpers Ferry, with its massive arms foundry, to its unenviable fate. The Federals, with the 9th New York in the forefront, fought their way methodically over South Mountain, carefully deploying to Lee's front.

On 17 September, the armies of Lee and McClellan joined battle south of Antietam Creek. Despite his massive numerical advantage (Union soldiers outnumbered the Confederates by nearly two to one), McClellan refused to commit his troops in a single concerted attack and thus probably denied them total victory. After the battle, in which the North lost an estimated 2,100 dead, 9,550 injured, and 750 captured against Confederate losses of 1,510 dead, 7,800 wounded, and 1,850 captured, Lee was forced to retire south rather than risk his lines of communication. Yet despite optimistic proclamations in Washington, Antietam was far from a Union victory, and a few days later McClellan was relieved of command.

In July 1862, the 9th New York Volunteers were belatedly issued with the .58 caliber Springfield rifle-musket in lieu of their outdated smoothbores. In all, over 700,000 "1861 Springfields" were manufactured before mass production ceased in 1863; a quarter of a million of these were made in the Springfield armory itself, the rest by outside contractors. Equipped with a simple hammer-and-nipple firing mechanism the new percussion Springfield with its maximum range of 1,000 yards (915m) revolutionized the battlefield.

The 9th New York was one of the few Zouave units to wear their uniforms throughout their period of enlistment. Officers were issued with formal Zouave dress uniform including a dark blue shako adorned with a bushy white plume, but they tended to wear more conventional dress in the field. In line with most "Americanized" units, the enlisted men's uniform was principally of the Zouave pattern but with dark blue *chasseur* trousers. A regulation sky blue overcoat was worn over a dark blue jacket and undershirt, the whole relieved by a magenta trim, magenta or light blue rank chevrons, and a turquoise or blue sash. A scarlet fez with a blue tassel was issued but invariably replaced by a soft, dark red, woolen cap. The *chasseur* trousers were of the same cloth as the jacket. Cut full at the pleated waist, they tapered to cuffs below the knee and were closed with buckles or buttons. Twelve-inch (30cm) white gaiters, originally made of russet leather but later often constructed from pigskin or even canvas, were worn over the conventional black boots.

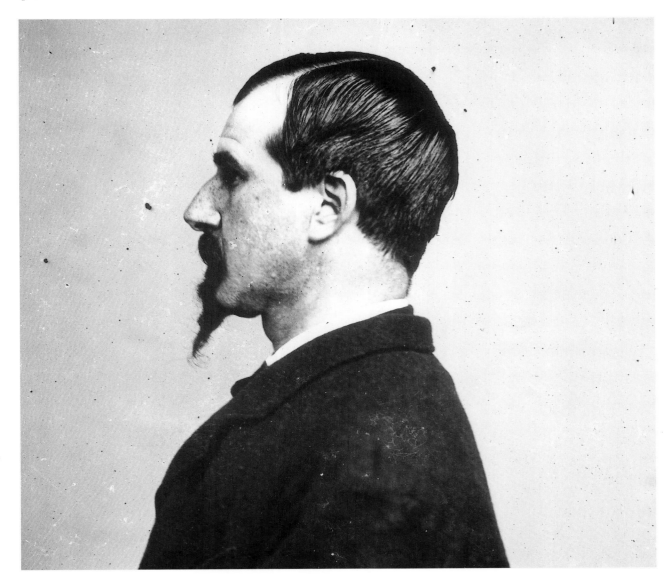

Rush Christopher Hawkins, commander of the 9th New York Volunteers.

39TH NEW YORK VOLUNTEER INFANTRY REGIMENT (GARIBALDI GUARD)

By 1861, Italy had scarcely resolved the question of its own unification and was in no position to influence the destiny of a faraway country with which it had few ties. Giuseppe Garibaldi had just declared Victor Emmanuel King of Italy, but Rome remained apart and aloof, its independence assured by the presence of powerful elements of the French army. Few Italians looked beyond the Mediterranean for inspiration and even fewer emigrated. Those who did rarely exported their political ideals, preferring to work hard and merge themselves into their new society. Consequently Italian settlers in the United States suffered little of the bigotry felt so keenly by the more volatile Irish and southern Germans crammed into the slums of the northeastern seaboard cities. Instead the community spread southward and westward, integrating well wherever it attempted to lay down new roots.

Not surprisingly, therefore, many Italians who volunteered their services to the Union at the outbreak of war happily followed their neighbors into local militias rather than attempting to form expatriate units. Such Italian regiments as were formed were often only superficially authentic. The 39th New York Volunteer Infantry Regiment – the Garibaldi Guard – was typical. Although dressed in uniforms virtually identical to those worn by the crack riflemen and sharpshooters of the Bersaglieri Light Infantry, the regiment in fact consisted of three companies of Germans, three of Hungarians, one each of Swiss, Italians, and Frenchmen and a composite company of Spanish and Portuguese immigrants.

Raised by the Union Defense Committee of the Citizens of New York simultaneously with the 40th, 41st, and 42nd New York Volunteers in response to an urgent Presidential call for more troops, the regiment was formed on conventional pre-war lines.

It was commanded by a colonel with a lieutenant colonel as second-in-command. Headquarters consisted of a major, two lieutenants acting as adjutant and quartermaster, a surgeon, his assistant, a commissary sergeant, a hospital steward, two principal musicians, and 24 bandsmen. (Soon after its formation, the Garibaldi Guard gained considerable unwelcome notoriety when its first colonel-in-chief, Frederick George D'Utassey, was convicted of fraud, cashiered and sent to Sing Sing prison.)

In bivouac, the band, which contained few accomplished musicians and whose playing was more often described as spirited than tuneful, acted as a general support, providing guards or music as the need arose. In battle, however, its members took on the far more crucial and dangerous role of stretcher bearers, transporting the wounded from the battlefield to the comparative safety of the regimental dressing station. Although few bandsmen were decorated for bravery, many earned the uncompromising respect of men whose lives they had saved.

President Lincoln and General Scott review the Garibaldi Guards prior to their leaving for the front line.

Hat: The black brimmed hat, adorned with the letters "GG" in gold and a flowing plume, bore witness to the regiment's Bersaglieri traditions.

Tunic: The *chasseur*-style tunics with their pleated flared skirts and red piping were largely replaced in 1863 by standard New York-issue blue.

Weapons: Most troops were armed with the 1841 "Mississippi" rifle capable of accuracy at great range.

GARIBALDI GUARD!

PATRIOTI ITALIANI!
HONVEDEK!
AMIS DE LA LIBERTE!
DEUTSCHE FREIHEITS KÆMPFER!

APPEAL!

The aid of every man is required for the service of his ADOPTED COUNTRY! A Regiment of Riflemen, Bersaglieri, Honvedek, Chasseurs, or Scharfschutzen, is now formed under the name of the GARIBALDI GUARD, and encamped near Washington. This Regiment will be increased by order of Government to 1150.

Wanted at once,

250 ABLE-BODIED MEN!

Italians, Hungarians, Germans, and French, Patriots of all Nations,

AROUSE! AROUSE! AROUSE!

The Families of our Soldiers shall be cared for.

PER ORDER.

Col. F. G. D'UTASSY,
Lieut. Col. A. REPETTI,
Maj. GEO. H. WARING, Jr.

Quartermaster, CHAS. B. NORTON.

Headquarters, Irving Building, 594 & 596 Broadway.

A stirring recruiting poster which helped to swell the ranks of the Garibaldi Guard.

Each of the ten companies was commanded by a captain supported by a lieutenant and second lieutenant. Theoretically it contained 98 enlisted men: a first sergeant, four sergeants, eight corporals, two musicians, a wagoner and 82 privates. However, within a year, due to the inexplicable Union habit of not drafting battle replacements into existing regiments but instead utilizing them to form new units, many of the companies were below half strength.

Two of the ten companies were designated flank companies. They were given additional light infantry training to enable them to operate forward of the main body prior to close contact with the enemy, at which time they would fall back to their designated flank. Most regiments chose their best and fittest marksmen for this role, but the sheer problems of language in so cosmopolitan an outfit as the 39th would have made this impossible. Furthermore, rifled muskets with which the regular flank companies were supposed to be armed were in such short supply in the early stages of the war that they would not have been available to the majority of line volunteer regiments. Flank troops therefore would have carried conventional smoothbore muskets no better than those equipping the massed ranks of the enemy facing them; denied the advantage of greater range and accuracy, they must have found their task suicidal.

Unusually the 39th was armed almost exclusively with the Model 1841 United States rifle. Known affectionately as the "Mississippi," in memory of Jefferson Davis's 1st Mississippi Regiment which used it to such good effect in 1847, or more commonly as the "*Jäger*" after the German huntsmen and light infantry units which pioneered its design, the rifle was considered one of the finest of its day. Manufactured originally as a .54 caliber percussion cap weapon, it was $48\frac{3}{4}$ inches (124cm) in total length and weighed about $9\frac{3}{4}$ lb (4.4kg). The seven-grooved barrel was fitted with a brass blade foresight and fixed rearsight then considered adequate for all purposes. Originally designed to accept a paper cartridge and spherical lead ball, most rifles were modified to .58 caliber to accept the hollow-based and far more accurate Minié bullet after its introduction in 1850.

Uniquely for a general-purpose weapon, there was no provision on the original models for a bayonet. However, the weapons were altered and equipped with a somewhat basic though effective rearsight and various mounts for a fiercesome $22\frac{1}{2}$ inch (145cm) saber bayonet. Despite the obvious potential of the weapon in hand-to-hand combat, however, the bayonet remained unpopular with the infantry of both sides, who preferred to use the rifle as a club rather than as a pike in close-quarter fighting. It is quite possible therefore that many members of the 39th would have conveniently "lost" their unusually heavy and inconvenient saber bayonets on the first available occasion.

As part of the 3rd Brigade, 3rd Division, II Corps, Army of the Potomac, the regiment was surrendered at Harpers Ferry on 15 September 1862 but was later exchanged in time to serve at Gettysburg, in the Wilderness campaign, and at Spotsylvania and Petersburg before being mustered out at the beginning of July 1865.

Although the surrender of Harpers Ferry was ignominious for the North, it should not be seen as a reflection of the fighting potential of the 39th Regiment nor indeed of any of the approximately 12,000 men comprising the garrison. Situated at the junction of the Shenandoah and Potomac rivers and dominated on three sides by high ground, the town's very position frustrated its effective defense. Besieged as a prelude to the Battle of Antietam (Sharpsburg), the outpost was surrounded by 27,000 battle-hardened Southern troops under the command of the redoubtable "Stonewall" Jackson. Confederate artillery was immediately placed on all the vantage points overlooking the Union camp and annihilation offered as the only alternative to surrender. Not realizing that Lee's Army of Northern Virginia was outnumbered and dangerously split, that McClellan was in possession of a detailed copy of the Confederate plan of campaign (found by a Union soldier wrapped around three cigars and passed immediately to army Headquarters), and that Jackson's men were required urgently elsewhere, the garrison commander felt that he had no option but to surrender his post, which was in the event of no strategic importance to the North. Neither he nor any of his subordinates were subsequently admonished for this decision.

The original uniform of the Garibaldi Guard was distinctly nationalistic. Whereas the enlisted men were issued with relatively plain *chasseur*-style jackets adorned with a pleated flared "skirt" and red piping, many officers wore ornate gold frogging across their chests and relieved the drabness of their blue jackets with heavily braided cuffs and collars. Until the introduction of standard blue uniforms for all New York militia regiments in May 1863, all enlisted men and most officers in the 39th wore plain red wool flannel shirts above blue trousers tucked into black leather gaiters when operating in the field. A striking black brimmed hat, adorned with the letters "GG" in gold and complemented by a flowing green plume attached to the left of the chin strap button, completed the outfit.

Colonel Frederick d'Utassey, the first commander of the Garibaldi Guard, dressed in formal uniform.

79TH NEW YORK (HIGHLANDERS)

The 79th New York (Highland) Volunteer Regiment was unique in many respects. On the face of it a conventional militia unit, it in fact owed its structure and many of its traditions to the British army in which a number of its officers and men had seen previous service. Spurred on by hunger and economic deprivation, many Scots had emigrated to the New World in the 1850's. Unlike their Irish counterparts, they had not brought with them a deep-seated hatred of Britain but instead had continued the maintainance of close and friendly links with the homeland. Dour, religious, and, above all, industrious, many had become lynchpins of local society.

By the mid-19th century, Scots' prowess on the battlefield was universally respected. Against Napoleon, a lone piper had rallied the wavering lines of Redcoats at Quatre Bras, turning potential defeat into assured victory, and a few hours later at Waterloo, the Highland brigade had swept all

French resistance before it. In the Crimea, oblivious to their own losses Highlanders had stormed the heights of Alma and had subsequently held the famous "thin red line" against overwhelming odds. It is not surprising therefore that, when New York State began to increase the size of its militia, the introduction of a Scots unit was heavily mooted, and when Captain Roderick of the British Consulate in New York City suggested on 9 October 1859 that a unit be formed based on an existing Highland regiment, the idea was readily adopted. The British regiment chosen for the honor was the 79th (the Cameron Highlanders), today amalgamated into the Queen's Own Highlanders (Seaforth and Camerons) but then a fiercely independent regiment with an uncompromising reputation and an enviable array of battle honors.

Initially, the Union 79th was formed into four exclusively expatriate companies. However, when it was called into Federal service on 18 May 1861, its

Lt-Colonel Morrison of the 79th New York Highlanders on the parapet of the Tower Battery, James Island, South Carolina.

24

Headdress: Initially all ranks wore the traditional Glengarry of the Cameron Highlanders, but as the war progressed this was increasingly replaced by the conventional Union blue cap.

Kilt: A few diehards continued to wear the Cameron of Erracht kilt throughout the war. Most however succumbed to practicality, relegating it to formal wear only.

Dirk: Worn sheathed in the right sock, the dirk, a short vicious fighting knife, proved devastating in close quarter action. Officers, N.C.O.s and bandsmen were armed with a long straight sword, other ranks with the bayonet.

strength was increased to the conventional ten companies and 1,000 officers and men by the introduction of Scottish, Irish, and English New Yorkers along with a few of other nationalities. Despite this, great care was taken not to compromise the Scottish identity of the regiment. A pipe and drum band – an integral part of any Scottish regiment – was formed and proved so proficient that, within weeks of the outbreak of war, it was seconded to the White House for Presidential duties. Despite the obvious honor this bestowed upon the regiment, it did have its disadvantages, not least because it deprived the unit of stretcher bearers, which was the duty of bandsmen in battle. It was a perennial complaint of company commanders that their best men were frequently taken away from front-line service to undertake regimental and other duties, and in this instance, the place of the bandsmen would have had to be taken by much needed infanteers.

Initially, as befitted a Scottish regiment, the 79th wore a most distinctive uniform. In full dress, soldiers wore a traditional Highland doublet adorned with red shoulder straps bearing the numbers "79" engraved in brass. Red cuff-patches with light blue piping and a collar which was usually red edged with light blue but occasionally light blue with a red and white patch provided contrast without gaudiness. The whole was completed by rear tails carrying embroidered twin yellow exploding grenades. A blue Glengarry cap with a red bobble and red-and-blue tartan hat strap was worn with the dress uniform, but this was replaced in the field by a conventional Union-issue blue cap. Originally a large brass regimental badge was worn on the Glengarry, but as the conflict progressed, tradition succumbed to financial expediency and a simpler replica of the New York State seal was substituted.

The kilt, the very epitome of the British Highland regiment, was issued and usually worn as part of the formal dress, although occasionally it was replaced by trews, a form of heavily decorated plaid trousers more usually associated with the Scottish Lowlands. The kilt was made of cloth woven into the Cameron of Erracht tartan, similar to that of the sister British regiment. A heavy white-hair sporran with twin black horsehair tails and a white metal thistle badge secured by a thin black leather strap were worn to the front. Red-and-white checkered, knee-length, woolen socks with red gaiters, black leather shoes, silver shoe buckles, and a fiercesome curved knife, worn sheathed in the right sock and known as a "dirk," completed the formidable uniform.

N.C.O.s wore red sashes, yellow epaulettes, and light blue chevrons. The long, straight, traditionally Scottish sword issued to all officers, N.C.O.s, and bandsmen was secured in a black scabbard attached to a leather belt with a gilt, 2-inch (5cm) wide rectangular buckle embossed with a silver wreath of laurel and palm encircling the Old English letters "sny." Bayonets, which varied in design according to the weapon carried, but which on average were $38\frac{1}{2}$ inches (98cm) long, were issued to the private soldiers who, unlike so many of their Union compatriots, proved on more than one occasion that they were not afraid to use them.

Traditionally, the 79th elected its officers. Colonel James Cameron, the brilliant and charismatic brother of the self-seeking and far less worthy Secretary of War, was chosen to lead the regiment into its baptism of fire at the 1st Battle of Manassas (Bull Run), during which tragically he and 197 of his troops were killed. When Isaac Ingalls Stevens was appointed in his place without the regiment's prior approval, a minor bloodless mutiny occurred as a result of which the 79th was stripped of its colors.

Stevens, who eventually became extremely popular with his men, was an experienced military engineer, politician, and explorer. An expert on Indian affairs, he had been severely criticized in the past for his placatory attitude toward the Plains Indians whom many of his colleagues regarded as their natural enemy. He was a member of the House of Representatives from 1857 until he assumed command of the 79th on 30 July 1861. Promoted brigadier general the following September and major general on 4 July 1862, he was given command of 1st Division, IX Corps (which included the Highlanders) and was killed at Chantilly, Virginia during the 2nd Battle of Manassas, with the recently restored regimental colors in his hands, having rescued them from the sixth standard bearer to have fallen. A short and rather stout man with a massive head, Stevens was described as dignified and humorless. Yet he was an officer of great potential and, at the

time of his death, was being considered as the next commander of the Army of the Potomac.

In all, the 79th served with distinction in 59 engagements before it was mustered out on 13 May 1864 (after which men with unexpired terms formed two companies of the New Cameron Highlanders). It lost 110 officers and men from a total of 474 engaged at the Battle of James Island and 105 at 2nd Manassas, after which its colors were restored in recognition of its valiant conduct.

At no time did the 79th demonstrate the true tenacity of the Highlander more than at the 1st Battle of Manassas. Arguably the most obscene destroyer of American idealism of all time, this battle – called Bull Run by the North and Manassas by the Confederacy – should never have been fought. Green troops, often dressed in gaudy uniforms more befitting the ballroom than the battlefield and armed with rifles and muskets few of them could handle, clashed in a bloody battle demanded by the politicians and dreaded by the generals. The battle itself was neither big nor decisive. The Union fielded an army of 35,000 and the Confederacy 32,500, yet such was the rawness of the battalion officers and the ineptitude of the staff that only 18,572 Northerners met 18,053 Southerners in actual combat. Light by later standards, the casualty lists nevertheless seemed dreadful at the time: the Union sustained 2,896 casualties includ-

ing 460 dead, and the Confederacy 1,982 casualties of whom 387 were fatalities. Initially all went well for McDowell's Northerners as they relentlessly pushed the (at that stage) heavily outnumbered Southern troops back from the sluggish waters of Bull Run itself up onto Henry House Hill. However, the Confederate General Beauregard, anticipating the central axis of the Federal attack, brought up reserves and began to turn the Union tide. Stagnation in the latter's advance turned to indecision and quickly to fear as many of the "90-day" troops comprising the bulk of the Washington army, their three-month term almost up, fell back. As inexperienced officers lost control and men became separated from their friends, fear turned to panic and a withdrawal to a rout until the greater part of the army was retreating to the protective defenses of Washington.

As the majority of Federal troops discarded their guns, packs, and anything else which might impede their escape, a few units maintained their discipline, slowing and disorganizing the Confederate pursuit. Many of these units were regulars but others were volunteers, mainly from Sherman's brigade. Of these, few fought more bravely than the 79th New Yorkers, proving to the world that their tenacity and fighting ability as well as their uniforms were a match for their venerated Highland ancestors.

General Kearney leads the charge at the Battle of Chantilly.

U.S. COLORED INFANTRY

No event has so affected black people in the United States as did the Civil War. Contrary to popular opinion, however, slavery was a catalyst and never a cause of the war. Lincoln realized early that precipitate action against slavery would compromise the neutrality of the border states, would undermine his position in the North where anti-Negro feelings were running high and would make virtually impossible his overriding aim to save the Union. As late as August 1862, Lincoln confided in the influential anti-slavery editor Horace Greeley that "If I could save the Union without freeing any slave, I would do it; and if I could save it by freeing all the slaves, I would do it; and if I could save it by freeing some and leaving others alone, I would do that."

Surprisingly perhaps, by mid-1862 Lincoln had already decided privately to issue a proclamation of emancipation and was only awaiting a suitable time for its publication. The war was going badly for the North. The Confederacy had been able to release the bulk of its fit young men for front-line combat, relying on its 3.5 million slaves for the production of food, raw materials and ammunition without which it would have found it impossible to survive the first winter. Its armies had seized the initiative early on, winning a series of swift vic-

tories which threw the North into a crisis of self-doubt and recrimination. Ominously the British government, if not its people, were showing signs of a distinct bias toward the South.

Abolitionists advised strongly that, were Lincoln to introduce emancipation, he would elevate the war to the level of a social crusade. Emancipation would be followed by a groundswell of unrest among the Southern slaves, possibly leading to sporadic insurrection. Furthermore, Britain would certainly be deterred from direct intervention on the side of slavery against freedom.

Union army generals remained ambivalent toward the question of slavery. Some relied on the provisions of the Fugitive Slave Law of 1850 to return escapees to their masters, ignoring completely the fact that the society from which they had fled was now at war with the North. Others, notably General Benjamin Butler commanding troops on the Virginia coast, deemed all slaves "contraband of war" and put them to work for the Federal cause. In August 1861, Congress passed the Confiscation Act, empowering the authorities to seize all property employed "in aid of the rebellion," including "contrabands," as a result of which thousands of ex-slaves found themselves working for the downfall of their former masters. None,

54th Massachusetts (Colored) Regiment storming Fort Wagner, 3 July 1863.

Kepi: Many Colored Infantry wore black waterproofs over their otherwise conventional blue kepis.

Frock coats: Many units formed later in the war were issued with excellently tailored dress uniforms including the traditional frock coat which most wore with the collar down.

Units retained for garrison duty might be expected to parade in their full packs as depicted here. "Fighting" troops would usually contrive to lose much of the unnecessary kit.

During 1862, a series of enactments forbade the return of fugitive slaves, abolished slavery within the District of Columbia, prohibited its practice in Federal territories and ultimately freed all slaves in the Confederacy. Lincoln delayed the formal Proclamation of Emancipation until September 1862 by which time the Union army had gained a crushing victory at Antietam (Sharpsburg). In so doing, he carefully obviated any suggestion that the law was being changed simply to provide cannon fodder.

Whereas the Proclamation made little immediate difference to the slaves still under Confederate sovereignty, it did offer them great hope for the future. News of the Proclamation spread by word of mouth among the slaves who at last realized the potential of a Union victory.

The inevitable migration to the Northern industrial cities of thousands of freed and escaped slaves brought serious social unrest which occasionally manifested itself in openly racist rioting. Attempts

Although this photograph is obviously posed, it demonstrates clearly the high standard of uniform issued to black troops during the latter stages of the war.

by Lincoln to mitigate the problem through the medium of black emigration failed in the face of mushrooming black patriotism. Increasingly, black Americans were demanding the right to fight for their new country.

The United States navy, which had traditionally accepted men of all races, recruited an estimated 20,000 blacks during the Civil War. Although the majority were confined to the anonymity of the lower decks, a few obtained fame and promotion, none more so than Captain Robert Smalls of the *Planter* who daringly sailed his ship under the guns of the Charleston shore batteries to join the blockading Union fleet.

By the winter of 1862, the Federal government had committed itself to emancipation. Despite the bravery of their brothers in the navy and the increasing eloquence of men such as Frederick Douglass, himself an escaped slave and now an influential lecturer and author, Lincoln continued to doubt the potential military value of ex-slaves. Not only did he fear that the loyal border states would be affronted at the sight of ex-slaves bearing arms against their "natural" masters, but he also doubted that blacks, particularly ex-plantation workers, would have the confidence to face in close-quarter battle those whom for generations they had been taught to fear and defer to.

By September 1862, however, the Northern situation was critical. Few of the 300,000 volunteers called for in July had materialized and the army was now far below strength. Against his better judgment, Lincoln at last agreed to the necessity for black regiments. Ben Butler raised the Corps d'Afrique (Louisiana Native Guards), and on 27 September 1862, his 1st Louisiana National Guard became the first black regiment to be mustered into Federal service. The 2nd Louisiana National Guard was formed a month later, and the 3rd and 4th in November. At about that time, General David Hunter, a veteran of the Indian and Mexican wars, sanctioned the formation of the 1st South Carolina Volunteers from freed slaves in the areas of the Carolinas and Georgia then under Union control. Inspired by their enlightened commander, the Massachusetts abolitionist Thomas Wentworth Higginson, the South Carolinas distinguished themselves in a number of early skirmishes with Confederate platoons, encouraging their leader to report, that "no officer in this regiment now doubts that the key to the successful prosecution of this war lies in the unlimited employment of black troops." Convinced, Lincoln immediately ordered the implementation of full-scale black enlistment. The President's initial demand for four black regiments was soon overtaken by events, and by August 1863, 14 black regiments – 14,000 troops in all – were in the field or ready for deployment, with another 24 in the process of forming.

On 27 May 1863, two Louisiana regiments became the first black troops to participate in a general engagement when they led the assault on the Confederate stronghold at Port Hudson, Louisiana, on the Mississippi. Although unsuccessful, such was the nature of their bravery that all but the most stalwart of conservatives were forced to concede that the commitment of such troops was now beyond doubt. On 7 June 1863, the raw and untried black garrison at Milliken's Bend, Louisiana held its position in hand-to-hand combat against the veterans of General Walker's division. On 18 July, the 54th Massachusetts, the first black regiment to be recruited in the North, led an attack on Battery Wagner overlooking Charleston harbor. Out of a total of 650 engaged, the regiment lost 272 wounded and killed, (including its commanding officer), but although unsuccessful, it at once won itself the universal respect of Union and Confederate leadership alike. Prominent politicians who had once sneered at the idea of black soldiers were forced to admit their worth, and Lincoln at once accelerated their enlistment.

As Union forces advanced deeper into Southern territory, they gathered more able-bodied blacks into their ranks until, by 1865, there were a total of 166 regiments – 145 infantry, 7 cavalry, 12 heavy artillery, 1 field artillery and 1 engineer – of which approximately 60 had experienced combat. Thirty-eight regiments participated in the invasion of Virginia while others led the advance into Charleston and Richmond – a final humiliation for the defenders. Few black troops fought in more than one major battle. Nevertheless, of the 178,895 who enlisted and were deployed in the 449 engagements in which black troops were involved, over 3,700 lost their lives. This is a massive number when it is remembered that black troops fought only in the latter half of the war.

Seventeen black soldiers and four sailors were awarded the Congressional Medal of Honor, the highest accolade of a grateful government.

Black troops did not receive special uniforms, although their smartness on parade was commented on by more than one senior officer. However, whether this was due to the fact that many were employed on garrison duties where standards were easier to maintain or whether it was due to a higher level of regimental *élan* remains a moot point. Many of the regiments that formed late in the war were equipped with uniforms made of high-quality cloth rather than the conventional serge which was in short supply at the time, a factor which greatly enhanced their appearance.

Negro soldiers, among the most devout in the Federal army, attend an impromptu religious service.

OFFICER: U.S. CORPS OF ENGINEERS

At the outbreak of war, the United States army boasted two highly efficient but independent establishments: the Corps of Engineers, responsible for the planning, supervision, construction, and maintenance of the network of railroads, roads, canals, and bridges mushrooming throughout the country; and the Corps of Topographical Engineers, responsible for the provision and updating of maps. In 1863, in recognition of their complementary nature, the two corps were amalgamated into a single Corps of Engineers consisting of 105 officers and 752 enlisted men.

Battlefield surveys, although often far from accurate, were vital to the planning of the war, particularly as many engagements took place in areas which had never been properly mapped. There were problems reproducing these in sufficient quantities. Initial attempts at photographing maps at the front met with limited success due to the distortion caused by the varying focal lengths of the primitive lenses employed. High-quality maps could be produced by lithography, but this was demanding of men and materials and had therefore to be carried out well behind the front line. For quick repro-

duction, maps were drawn on thin sheets of cloth, stretched over a silver nitrate-sensitized sheet and held up to the sunlight. The lower sheet was then "fixed," resulting in a map comprising white lines on a black background. Although such primitive reproductions soon faded, they usually proved adequate for the task required and had the benefit of being easily replaceable.

The Topographic Engineers also reconnoitered routes, from the point of view of potential enemy movement as well as that of friendly forces, taking particular account of the strength and location of bridges, the nature of the railroads, and the adequacy of food and water supplies. In this respect, they were among the first true "intelligence" troops.

The Union army was well endowed with officers competent in engineering and therefore found no difficulty in expanding the Corps as circumstances demanded. Knowledge at the time was comparatively primitive, lacking the exactitude which marks present undertakings. Sophisticated equipment simply did not exist, the majority of works being undertaken with the traditional pick and

U.S. Engineers constructing a landing stage at Belle Plain, Virginia in May 1864. Note the informal inscription in the foreground.

Headdress: Officers wore a standard black dress hat with a brass cap badge denoting a castle with a sally port in front and turrets on either side. Even after their amalgamation in 1863, many Topographical Engineers continued to wear their traditional cap badge denoting a gold shield within a wreath.

Tunic: Branch of service was denoted by black shoulder tabs and gold trouser cords. Once again Topographical Engineers tended to wear buttons denoting a shield above the old English letters "T.E."

shovel. Never was the maxim "Soldier first and specialist second" more true than with the engineers, whose front-line involvement often brought them into direct contact with the enemy to the extent that the Corps actually fought as infantry at the Battle of Malvern Hill in Virginia (1 July 1862).

A number of states raised their own independent troops. New York raised the 1st Engineer Regiment (Serrell's Engineers) which operated along the South Carolina coast. It eventually participated in the siege of Petersburg, together with the 15th and 50th Engineer Regiments, both formerly infantry units, which, together with the 1st U.S. Engineer Battalion, provided brigade support for the Army of the Potomac. Missouri raised Bissell's Engineer Regiment, which amalgamated in 1864 with the 25th Missouri Infantry to form the 1st Missouri Engineer Regiment, while Michigan raised a further regiment and Kentucky and Pennsylvania independent companies.

The primary role of the Corps of Engineers in wartime – the construction of defenses and fortifications – grew considerably in importance as each side obtained bigger and heavier artillery and mastered the art of mounting huge siege mortars on floating rafts. Traditionally, fire trenches and gun emplacements were designed by engineers but constructed by the infantry destined to occupy them. However, as the war progressed units of pioneers were introduced to take over the actual construction work to allow the hard-pressed infantry a modicum of rest between actions.

Pre-war coastal forts, designed on classical European principles, tended to be large, masonry affairs invariably pentagonal in shape and occasionally with protruding bastions. Many had two or three floors of guns. Although presenting an enormous target, the forts relied on their overwhelming firepower to annihilate an enemy fleet before the latter could sail close enough to return effective fire. Ships, it was argued, were not steady firing platforms and accurate targeting was virtually impossible. Fortresses, on the other hand, with their stability and protection, could concentrate fire onto a single target with devastating effect. Land approaches were protected by traditional water-filled ditches and outworks.

The Civil War heralded the advent of powerful new artillery pieces which obviated the need for the traditional coastal assault. Forts once considered impregnable now found themselves at the mercy of long-range rifled ordnance, small and light enough to be moved across land. The death knell for the traditional fortification was convincingly sounded on 11 April 1862 when the 40 casemated guns of Fort Pulaski (outside Savannah, Georgia) were battered into submission by Federal rifled artillery standing off nearly two miles from their target. Where possible, all future fortifications were constructed with sloping earthen ramparts to absorb and, if possible, deflect incoming shells.

Field fortifications, which soon proliferated on the battlefield, varied in dimensions and complexity, from simple shell scrapes dug with nothing more advanced than the standard infantry bayonet to vast gun emplacements. Most began life simply and were gradually strengthened as time went on

by the addition of revetments, shelters, and listening and sentry posts. At one point, 68 minor forts interconnected by 20 miles of trenches surrounded Washington D.C.

Responsibility for the strengthening of the major fortifications passed to the Corps of Engineers. Fields of fire were made to interlock; mines consisting of artillery shells or mortar bombs detonated by a basic percussion fuze were strewn; and obstacles in the form of pits, sharpened staves, and felled trees were strategically placed to slow the enemy advance.

Engineers tasked with the storming of enemy fortifications relied largely on the traditional method of "sap and parallel." The attacking forces first laid out their own lines well clear of the defender's artillery in such a way as to deny him reinforcements and replenishment. Zig-zag trenches, or "saps," were then excavated toward the enemy defenses. While still some distance from the enemy lines, the

saps were halted and linked by a consolidating trench or "parallel." Heavy artillery was then brought forward and the position strengthened. New saps were dug toward the positions of greatest vulnerability within the enemy front line and were eventually used as a staging point for a night assault. The carnage resulting from such attacks can only be imagined.

Bridging, both of rivers and of land obstacles, constituted one of the most important duties of the Corps, particularly in the latter stages of the war when the Union found it necessary to move huge armies over hostile territory. In his "march to the sea," General Sherman allotted each of his four corps a detachment of engineers equipped with a pontoon train offering bridging facilities of 900 ft (275m). Two such trains combined, it was argued, would be capable of crossing any river east of the Mississippi. Inevitably, bridging trains, with their vast array of heavy and complex equipment, could not always sustain the rapid rate of advance of unencumbered infantry, with the result that, where possible, the latter would often construct makeshift bridges from available resources rather than run the risk of losing the initiative through delay.

Engineer officers wore the standard officer's dress with black shoulder tabs and gold trouser cords to denote the branch of service. The cap badge – a brass castle with a sally port in front and turrets at each side (still proudly worn by the modern Corps) – was worn on a black dress hat. Prior to the amalgamation, Topographical Engineers wore a cap badge consisting of a gold shield within a wreath and buttons depicting a shield above the Old English letters "TE." After 1863, many Topographical Engineers continued to retain the old insignia, and indeed to refer to themselves by their traditional name. Enlisted men wore the plain fatigue uniform, although provision did exist for the issue of white coveralls in the field.

Far left: U.S. Engineers spent much of their time repairing bridges destroyed by the retreating Confederacy. Note the casualness of their uniforms.

Left: An officer of the U.S. Corps of Engineers, painted by H. Charles McBarron.

U.S. SHARPSHOOTERS

To be effective, sharpshooters – or "snipers" as they are known today – must be as skilled in fieldcraft as they are in marksmanship. They must be self-assured yet highly disciplined, and above all, they must be dedicated. Traditionally, the United States has always enjoyed a fine tradition of marksmanship, extending back to the woodsmen of the 18th century whose Kentucky and Pennsylvania long rifles scored such resounding successes against the British redcoats during the War of Independence. It is not surprising, therefore, that when Hiram Berdan set about the formation of the Sharpshooters on 30 November 1861, he was immediately inundated with volunteers.

The high minimum standards required – notably the ability to place ten consecutive rounds within the 10-inch (25cm) diameter of a bull's eye at 200 yards (185m) – plus the necessity for excellent references did, however, soon reduce the number of aspirants until, eventually, 1,392 officers and men were accepted into the ranks of the 1st Regiment. A further 1,178 all ranks enlisted into the 2nd Regiment when it was formed under the command of Colonel Henry Post soon after.

Berdan himself was a brilliant if unlovable indi-

The fine tradition of marksmanship in the United States produced many volunteer sharpshooters.

vidual. A mechanical engineer practicing in New York City at the outbreak of war, he had been the top rifle shot in the country for a staggering 15 years. Admired and therefore somewhat protected by General Winfield Scott, Berdan was nevertheless regarded as unscrupulous and untrustworthy by the vast majority of his peers. He nevertheless created in the Sharpshooters some of the most versatile and respected soldiers of the war.

Initially, the volunteers brought their own hunting rifles, but when this created acute problems of ammunition resupply, Berdan requested the universal issue of the coincidentally named Sharps rifle. James W. Ripley, the conservative and hot-tempered Chief of Ordnance, joined with Scott in insisting instead that Berdan's troops be issued with muzzle-loading Springfields. In making this decision, Ripley was merely mirroring the views of the majority of traditional military minds. The .52 caliber single-shot breechloading Sharps rifle was revolutionary in design and therefore expensive to produce at a time when financial saving was all-important. More fundamentally, it was feared that the additional ammunition expenditure would lead to insurmountable resupply problems. After per-

Tunic: All ranks were issued with dark green caps and jackets, the latter with black, non-shine, thermoplastic buttons to offer maximum camouflage.

Weapons: Despite initial objections from the Pentagon, from 1862 the Sharpshooters were issued with the deadly accurate Sharps rifle capable of picking off enemy artillerymen at ranges in excess of 800 yards.

Leggings: Black leather leggings were issued to all ranks but abandoned by most as unnecessarily cumbersome.

37

sonally witnessing a spectacular exhibition of marksmanship by Berdan, however, Lincoln personally intervened and the coveted Sharps were issued between May and June 1862.

Uniquely among volunteer units, the Sharpshooters constituted Federal rather than state troops, although they were in practice recruited on a local basis. Within the 1st Regiment, Companies "A," "B," "D," and "H" were drawn from New York, Companies "C," "I," and "K" from Michigan, "E" from New Hampshire, "F" from Vermont and "G" from Wisconsin. The smaller 2nd Regiment, which unusually was confined to eight rather than the orthodox ten companies, drew from Minnesota (Company "A"), Michigan (Company "B"), Pennsylvania (Company "C"), Maine (Company "D"), Vermont (Companies "E" and "F"), and New Hampshire (Companies "F" and "G").

Never trained to fight conventionally, the Sharpshooters were invariably deployed as skirmishers, usually in company strength. The 1st Regiment, which lost 546 killed and wounded in four years of fighting, acquitted itself well at the Battle of Mine Run, when it lost its commander Lieutenant Colonel Caspar Trepp who had only recently succeeded Colonel Berdan. It was active throughout the Peninsula campaign, particularly in the battle for Yorktown when its members used their sniping rifles to excellent effect, neutralizing Confederate gun batteries. Although the regiment was granted its wish and issued with the Sharps rifle soon thereafter, there is evidence to suggest that a few picked marksmen retained their original personal weapons.

In 1863, the regiment was transferred to III Corps and in 1864 to II Corps. It distinguished itself amid the bloodletting of Chancellorsville (1–4 May 1863), at which time its skirmishers wreaked havoc among the forward elements of the 23rd Georgia Regiment, and at Gettysburg where it did much to stabilize the confused position facing General Dan Sickles and III Corps in the area of the Emmitsburg Road.

Gettysburg did, however, demonstrate the dangers inherent in relying on a single unit for the provision of an overall picture of a battle. General Sickles, in command of III Corps, unnerved by the lack of immediate intelligence and fearful of a large enemy build-up to his front and left flank, dispatched four companies of Sharpshooters supported by the 3rd Maine Infantry Regiment to establish the exact position. Berdan's men made contact with and drove back the enemy skirmishers but then met stiff resistance in the area of Pitzer's Wood. Withdrawing in good order, Berdan immediately reported the presence of a large number of Confederates. Although the concept of size is notoriously subjective (there were, in fact, only three regiments of Wilcox's Alabama Brigade deployed), Sickles immediately assumed that his earlier premonitions were true and that he was actually facing an entire army thrust. He at once ordered an advance *en masse*, leaving his designated position and his flanks wide open. Only the sheer professionalism of his own troops, aided by the quick reaction of General Sykes when ordered to bring forward V Corps from the reserve by General Meade, averted a catastrophe.

The 2nd Sharpshooters served with the ill-fated McDowell's Corps during the Peninsula campaign but as such were held in reserve. At Antietam (Sharpsburg) (17 September 1862), they were unusually, and wastefully, deployed into line of battle as part of Phelp's Brigade (Hooker's I Corps), losing 66 men in what is generally agreed to have been the bloodiest day's fighting of the war. Thereafter the regiment served successfully with I, III, and II Corps, usually as part of Birney's Division and alongside its sister regiment the 1st Sharpshooters. Its heaviest losses occurred during the Wilderness campaign and at Spotsylvania where it sustained, respectively, 76 and 53 casualties. In all, the regiment lost 462 killed and wounded before its disbandment.

Not all Sharpshooters accepted the Sharps rifle. A few picked marksmen were issued with heavy and meticulously manufactured sniper's rifles, often equipped with telescopic sights. Properly maintained and loaded and in the hands of experts, such weapons were capable of consistent 20-round

12-inch (30cm) groups at ranges in excess of 880 yards (805m). Such weapons were invariably muzzle loading, often with a false muzzle to minimize friction from the ramrod.

As tactics progressed and the musket became obsolete, the infantry's marksmanship improved and the commanders began to find it less necessary to rely on skirmishers to disrupt the enemy front line. More fundamentally, experience was proving that skirmishing lines were simply too flimsy to withstand the sustained attack of massed rows of bayonet-wielding infantry. By 1864, therefore, the role of the Sharpshooter was considered largely over. In the autumn of that year, the 1st Regiment was merged into the 2nd, and in February 1865 the entire unit was disbanded.

Uniforms issued to officers and men alike were among the most unusual and practical of the war. Originally both regiments wore dark green coats and caps (the latter with a black ostrich plume), light blue trousers (soon replaced with more practical green garments), and leather leggings. With comfort at a premium, personal innovations were tolerated with particular regard to the leggings which many volunteers discarded, preferring simply to tuck their trousers into their long woolen socks. A gray felt great coat trimmed with green was issued but abandoned by most after the first winter rains due to its unfortunate habit of stiffening uncomfortably when wet. The regulation U.S. army fatigue uniform was generally worn in the field, often with the addition of a blue flannel jacket. Dark green chevrons and stripes were worn by all N.C.O.s and non-shine, black thermoplast buttons by all ranks. The cap badge consisted of crossed rifles with the letters "US" above and "SS" below.

In close-quarter action, some volunteers abandoned their knapsacks in favor of smaller, more conventional haversacks worn in conjunction with the standard-issue black leather belt with its distinctive "US"-emblazoned buckle. Others found the Prussian-designed, hair-covered calfskin knapsack with its externally slung cooking utensils and additional storage space to be both comfortable and practical.

As the war progressed, formal lines of skirmishers were replaced by single sharpshooters trained to work on their own initiative.

N.C.O.: U.S. CAVALRY

Prior to 1861, the cavalry was considered in the United States to be militarily unimportant. It had produced no great leaders, had none of the social connections of its European counterparts, and totally lacked political patronage. With a few exceptions, it was based in a series of primitive and isolated forts in the far West from which it eked out a lonely, celibate existence far from the public eye. Few among the hordes of European immigrants who swelled the cities of the northeastern seaboard in the 1840's and 1850's felt any affinity for the horse, with the result that those who did enlist in the army tended to join the infantry. Not surprisingly the cavalry became a magnet for uninspiring officers and social misfits.

At the outbreak of war, there were only five regular U.S. cavalry regiments: the 1st and 2nd Dragoons, the Mounted Rifles, and the 1st and 2nd Cavalry, each consisting of five squadrons of two troops. Early in 1861, a sixth regiment, the 3rd Cavalry, was authorized, and a further squadron, again with two troops, was added to each regiment. Soon thereafter the entire force was streamlined. The 1st Dragoons became the 1st Cavalry, the 2nd Dragoons and Mounted Rifles became the 2nd and 3rd Cavalry, while the original 1st, 2nd, and 3rd Cavalry were redesignated the 4th, 5th, and 6th Cavalry – a move sure to have caused resentment

among these ranks who were bound to have regarded their new names as a demotion. Troops were increased officially to 100 men, although many remained under strength.

A regiment was commanded by a full colonel assisted by a lieutenant colonel, three majors, an adjutant, a quartermaster, a commissary, and a regimental surgeon and his assistant. Each troop was led by a captain supported by a lieutenant, a second lieutenant, and a so-called supernumerary, or "third" lieutenant. Each regiment contained a sergeant major, a quartermaster sergeant, a commissary sergeant, a saddler sergeant, a blacksmith, and two hospital stewards. Besides its officers, each troop had a first sergeant, a quartermaster sergeant, five sergeants, eight corporals, two teamsters, two blacksmiths, one saddler, a wagoner and two musicians.

In mid-1863, the Union army at last conceded the superiority of the Confederate cavalry and undertook a fundamental reorganization of its own mounted forces. The rank of "supernumerary" was scrapped, troops were increased in size from 82 to 100 men, and squadrons were eliminated in favor of battalions of four troops each. Onerous escort duties and camp pickets, which until then had fallen to the cavalry, were delegated to more suitable troops, while the cavalry itself at last began to

The charge of the 5th Cavalry during the Battle of Gaynes Mill.

Headddress: Cavalry kepis were molded to individual preference. All however bore the crossed sabers, regimental numbering and squadron lettering which differentiated them from the infantry.

Saddle: The McClellan-pattern saddle was hardy but uncomfortable. A fully-laden trooper was forced to sit bolt upright, allowing him little grip on the flanks of his mount.

Weapons: A pistol was secured to the right of the leather belt, a saber to the left. Regular cavalrymen carried the U.S. Pistol Carbine Model 1855, the volunteers any of a wide variety of carbines.

Company J, of 6th Pennsylvania Cavalry, rest during maneuvers. The lances, seen stacked in the foreground, would eventually be abandoned as impractical.

practice the *manoeuvre en masse* which had made its European equivalent such a formidable fighting force. An unnamed Confederate officer confirmed the success of the new training by stating at the end of the war that: "During the last two years, no branch of the Army of the Potomac contributed so much to the overthrow of Lee's army as the cavalry, both that which operated in the Valley of Virginia and that which remained at Petersburg."

Each cavalry regiment carried a regimental standard some 2 ft 5 inches (74cm) long by 2 ft 3 inches (69cm) deep. On its blue background was depicted a spread eagle bearing a red, white, and blue Federal shield upon its breast and holding a branch of laurel and sheaf of arrows in its talons. Above and below the eagle were two scrolls, the upper inscribed "*E Pluribus Unum*" in black lettering, the lower bearing the regimental title. Prior to the restructuring in 1863, after which each troop was issued with a guidon bearing the stars and stripes, a designated troop corporal carried the individual troop guidon. Each swallow-tailed guidon consisted of a red upper half bearing the letters "US" in white and a white lower portion containing the troop identifying letter. They were flown from 9 ft (2.7m) long poles, surmounted by standard brass pike-heads. Whatever effect the sight of the unfurled guidons may have had on the morale of the attacking cavalry, their bearers must have known that all available enemy guns would be turned on

them and it is unlikely therefore that the "honor" of bearing the guidons would have been universally popular.

Cavalry uniform was as practical as possible and relatively comfortable. Although the broad-brimmed slouch hat was occasionally worn, most troops favored the more common fatigue or forage cap, distinguished from the conventional infantry apparel by a brass badge on the crown comprising crossed sabers beneath the regimental number and above the squadron (later battalion) letter. Contemporary photographs show that many variations in the cut of the cap were tolerated as was the growing of facial hair, the latter probably a concession to the need to put water for the horses before personal hygiene. The short shell jacket, which had been in issue since the 1830's and which the cavalry now shared with the light artillery, was originally trimmed in orange for the dragoons, green for the mounted rifles, and yellow for the cavalry. However, after the amalgamation of the six regiments into one, all wore yellow. Trousers, which were sky blue with a thick yellow stripe, were heavily reinforced in the seat and inner leg to prevent chafing during the hours spent in the saddle. Ordinary black shoes were issued but, wherever possible, were replaced by a far more practical pair of black boots worn either hidden under the trousers or thigh high in the manner of the 17th-century English cavalier. The universal black leather belt held a "hog-leg" revolver holster on the right with the butt-cover extending forward, small pouches for percussion caps and pistol ammunition to its front, and a sword scabbard on the left.

The standard saddle throughout the Federal cavalry, both regular and volunteer, was the McClellan pattern first introduced into service in 1858. The saddle tree was made of wood, either beech or poplar, with a leather seat over a black rawhide cover. The stirrups were of wood with leather hoods. The girth, known as a "cinch," contained a ring at either end connected to the pommel and cantle of the saddle. A large leather carbine holster ran diagonally on the right of the saddle. Saddle bags, a blanket roll, and a poncho were all standard and attached to the saddle by means of individual straps. Contemporary sources suggest that the cavalryman was forced to sit bolt upright and consequently could not exert much grip on the flanks of his mount. Surrounded as he was by bags of oats, blankets, coats, and weaponry, he must have looked strange when traveling fully laden.

The traditional cavalry weapon – the saber – came in two types: light and heavy. The light cavalry saber Model 1860 had a 41-inch (104cm) blade, was 1 inch (2.5cm) wide at the hilt and slightly curved. The guard was of brass in half-basket form, the grip was covered in black leather bound in brass wire, and the pommel was in the shape of a Phrygian helmet. The slightly heavier Model 1840 saber had a thicker blade – $1\frac{1}{4}$ inches (3cm) thick at the hilt – but was otherwise similar in design. Both were carried in a plain wrought-iron scabbard with two rings for attachment to the belt. During the war, the Federal government purchased 203,285 light and 189,114 heavy sabers, more than ample to fully equip its cavalry forces.

All troopers and non-commissioned ranks in the cavalry carried carbines. Although in essence a carbine was little more than a lighter and shorter version of the standard rifle-musket, in practice those issued initially to the regular cavalry bore no real resemblance to the latter. The U.S. pistol carbine Model 1855, of which only 8,000 were ever manufactured, was based on the standard Model 1855 single-shot .58 caliber pistol and was used exclusively by the regular cavalry. The weapon, which was carried in a purpose-built saddle holster, consisted of a long-barreled but otherwise conventional pistol and a second shoulder stock. Normally it was fired single handed but when extra accuracy was demanded or the weapon was fired when the rider was dismounted, the shoulder stock was fitted and the whole became an improvised carbine.

Sheridan's Cavalry charge the Confederate lines at Five Forks, Virginia, 1 April 1865.

43

THE IRISH BRIGADE

Between 1846 and 1854, more than 3 million immigrants, a large number of them Irish Catholics, flooded into the United States. Although a few were educated, most were rural workers attempting to escape the deprivations of a subsistence existence eked out in a land plagued with blight and famine. Not unnaturally, the population already ensconced on American shores, itself no more than 20 million strong and traditionally Protestant, grew fearful for its established ways. The Irish were forced into ghettos in the seaboard cities of New England, New York, Pennsylvania, and Maryland where it was felt that they would be easier to control. Abused by the political parties, they were encouraged to vote but given no control over their destiny. Many became introverted, returning to secret societies and Fenianism for an outlet. Most regarded themselves as anti-British first and Americans second.

Between 1861 and 1863, a further 180,000 Irish emigrated to the United States, and of these, over 100,000 enlisted in the Union army. Others, however, remained impervious to the needs of their new country, regarding the war in general, and the question of slavery in particular, with little sympathy. A crisis occurred in 1863 when the Union introduced conscription. Fueled by the blatantly discriminatory terms of the Enabling Act under which a man might avoid service by paying $300 (more than a year's pay for an unskilled worker) or hiring a substitute, and no doubt egged on by drink, a mob of New York Irish broke into the provost marshal's office, destroying the draft records and setting fire to the building. Looting followed, during which an unfortunate and totally innocent black man was beaten and burned to death. Order was only restored with the help of the militia who arrived four days later.

Sunday morning Mass was a ritual attended by virtually every officer and man of the Brigade. These particular troops are from the 69th New York Volunteers.

By no means all Irishmen avoided service, and indeed there is evidence to suggest that large numbers emigrated to the United States specifically to join the Union forces. Their reasons for doing so were, however, often complex. Whereas many joined out of loyalty to their new country, others enlisted simply to gain military experience for the future war against the British. As if to emphasize this fact, on at least one occasion Irishmen from both the Union and Confederate forces met in no man's land to hold a "neutral" Fenian meeting to discuss future tactics. In addition, in 1866, many of the participants captured in the unsuccessful Fenian invasion of Canada were found to be wearing Federal uniforms.

Not surprisingly for a ghetto people wary of outsiders, the Irish preferred to enlist in their own regiments with leaders whom they knew and trusted. Responsibility for raising the Irish Brigade with its massive New York nucleus therefore fell to Thomas Francis Meagher, an influential Irish-American who had been transported to Tasmania for sedition and treasonous activity by the British only to escape to the United States in 1852. No fool, Meagher had at once taken out citizenship papers and had thereafter embarked on a noteworthy career as a lawyer, lecturer, and newspaper editor. Commissioned into the rank of brigadier general in February 1862, he commanded the Irish Brigade which he himself had formed that winter, serving with it in the Peninsula campaign, at the 2nd Battle of Manassas (Bull Run), and at the battles of Antietam (Sharpsburg), Fredericksburg, and Chancellorsville before resigning in May 1863, when the brigade, having been decimated, ceased to function as an effective unit. In December of that year, Meagher was reappointed to his rank and given a series of administrative commands under Sherman. After the war, he was appointed temporary governor of Montana, a position which he held until 1867 when tragically he fell off the deck of a Missouri steamer and drowned.

The Irish Brigade itself, which formed part of the 1st Division, II Corps, was large by Union standards. Originally it consisted of the 63rd to 69th New York Volunteers, the 88th New York Volunteers, the 166th Pennsylvania, and the 29th Massachusetts. This last regiment was replaced by the 28th Massachusetts in late 1862. The 166th Pennsylvania was withdrawn in 1864 and replaced in September of that year by the 7th New York Heavy Artillery, by then "relegated" to an infantry role.

It is impossible in the space available to describe in detail the actions of each individual regiment. Typically the 69th New York fought throughout the war, re-enlisting in September 1864 at the end of its three years' service. It lost eight regimental color bearers at Bloody Lane during the Battle of Antietam, and 16 of its 18 officers and 112 of its 210 men at Fredericksburg. During that battle, a color sergeant was found dead, shot through the heart, with the regimental flag concealed wrapped around his body.

The 28th Massachusetts, formed from the Boston Irish in January 1862, transferred to the Brigade in

Kepi: Service-issue kepi was adorned with a red clover-leaf badge.

Service coat: Embossed with distinctive green collar and cuffs.

Many troops abandoned the issue knapsack, with its tendency to disintegrate in the wet, in favor of the traditional blanket roll seen here.

45

the November of that year. Known as the "*Faugh-a-Ballagh*" (Gaelic for "clear the way"), it had by then already seen action as part of Stevens' Division, IX Corps at 2nd Manassas, sustaining 234 casualties, and at Antietam where it lost a further 48 out of its remaining strength of fewer than 200. As part of the Irish Brigade, it was heavily engaged at Fredericksburg, sustaining 158 casualties out of 416 officers and men; during the Wilderness campaign, losing 115 out of 505; and at Spotsylvania, losing 110 men, half in a single attack. When the regiment was mustered out on 13 December 1864, it refused to die, re-enlisting its recruits and men into a consolidated battalion of five companies which served for the duration of the war.

It is indicative of the fighting spirit of the Irish Brigade that three of its five commanders were killed in action, all in Virginia: Colonel Patrick Kelly at Petersburg; Major General Thomas Smyth (while commanding another brigade) at Farmville; and Colonel Richard Byrnes at Cold Harbor.

It is generally considered that the brigade experienced its finest, and one of its bloodiest, hours during the battle for the stone wall at the base of Marye's Heights at Fredericksburg (13 December 1862).

Both in conception and execution, Fredericksburg was a catalogue of Union ineptitude. General Burnside – jovial, trusting but inexperienced in large-scale warfare – had just assumed command of the Army of the Potomac, replacing the popular and, in the opinion of many, badly treated McClellan. Lincoln at once pressed for action, demanding exploitation of the "victory" at Antietam. Burnside hurriedly organized the army into three grand divisions: the left under General Franklin; the center under General Hooker; and the right – containing Major General Darius Couch's II Corps with its Irish Brigade – under General Sumner.

Elements of Sumner's 'Right Grand Division' were ordered to advance south from the army's headquarters in Warrenton toward the largely evacuated city of Fredericksburg, with a view to crossing the Rappahannock River and proceeding south to Richmond. Initially, Lee was slow to realize Burnside's intentions and only belatedly ordered Longstreet to adopt a defensive position on Marye's Heights overlooking the river. Inexplicably, the Federals made no immediate attempt to cross into the virtually defenseless city but instead consolidated along the river's northern banks, allowing Lee ample time to prepare. Subsequent attempts to construct five pontoon bridges across the Rappahannock proved impossible due to the presence of 3,000 Mississippi sharpshooters positioned in buildings and slit trenches along the southern bank. Efforts by Union batteries to support the exposed engineers proved ineffectual, and it was not until Burnside ordered massed artillery fire onto the city, with its resultant confusion and carnage, that Union troops were able to cross in pontoon boats and dislodge the tenacious Confederates. Two days later, the bulk of Burnside's troops were across the river and in a position to assault Lee's by now excellently prepared positions.

After attempts by Franklin to probe the Confederate's right wing met with failure, Sumner was ordered to assault their center-left with its apex on the gently rising Marye's Heights. The Confederate position was formidable. Fresh troops were positioned four to six deep along a sunken road at the base of the hill, which was further protected by a stone wall along its forward edge. Artillery was dug into the rear, making a frontal assault virtually suicidal. Nevertheless Sumner's troops, with the Irish in the vanguard, charged no fewer than 14 times, rarely getting within 100 yards (91m) of the enemy position before being driven back. In all, 900 Union troops died in the futile assault on Marye's Heights, many of them from exposure as they lay wounded and freezing in no man's land. Two days later, dejected and defeated, Burnside withdrew the remnants of his shattered army north across the river. Major General Couch wrote of his friend Burnside that, after the battle, "he [Burnside] wished his body was also lying in front of Marye's Heights." The bodies of an undisclosed number of the Irish Brigade were. Yet unlike units endowed with less spirit, the brigade recovered and fought on throughout another vicious 18 months of war.

The Irish Brigade wore a distinctive uniform consisting of the regulation fatigue coat with the addition of green collar and cuffs, and gray trousers. A red clover-leaf badge adorned the top of the service kepi. To emphasize its national heritage, each regiment carried its own individual flag as well as its conventional state and regimental colors.

Facing page, top: The Irish Brigade experienced its finest hour during the carnage of Fredericksburg, when no fewer than 14 fruitless attempts were made to scale the Confederate stronghold on Marye's Heights.

Facing page, bottom: Few photographs show more clearly the slaughter of Bloody Lane.

Exhausted troops pose for a photograph during a respite in the battle for Bloody Lane.

GUNNER: UNION LIGHT ARTILLERY

Despite the steady growth in the importance of artillery throughout early 19th-century Europe, the pre-war Union army had largely failed to recognize the significance of this arm of service. The scale and establishment of ordnance had been laid down by the Secretary of War but this was largely ignored. Theoretically, one field piece was allotted per 1,000 infantrymen and two per 1,000 cavalry. Of this allocation two-thirds were guns, of which three-quarters were 6–pounders and the residue 12-pounders, and one-third were the less mobile howitzers with 12- and 24-pounders in the same ratio. Light artillery was organized into either horse or field batteries, each with six guns and either six or 12 ammunition wagons depending on the caliber of the weapons. The battery itself was subdivided into sections of two guns and an ammunition wagon, the whole commanded by a lieutenant. Six additional ammunition wagons were held in company reserve, as was a mobile forge and supply wagon. In the

A photograph for propaganda purposes only. In reality, few guns were manned by a full complement. The muskets, so clearly in evidence here, would rarely have been taken into action.

horse artillery, the crews of nine were mounted, but the rest were expected to walk or hitch lifts on the support vehicles. Guns were invariably allocated piecemeal along the entire battle front, there being no centralized plan for their concerted use.

After the disaster of the 1st Battle of Manassas/ Bull Run (21 July 1861), immediate steps were taken to reorganize the artillery. Wherever possible, the six guns within each battery were standardized, considerably relieving the problems of resupply; batteries were reallocated on the scale of four per division, at last making it possible to bring down concentrated fire on a single point; and divisional artillery assets were placed under the command of a regular army captain. For added versatility, a mobile reserve of 100 light guns was created and placed in the rear.

It is testament to the organizational ability of Major (later Brigadier General) William Farquhar Barry, tasked with the rebuilding of the artillery,

Headdress: At the outset of hostilities most Union gunners were professional soldiers attached to regular army units with long traditions borrowed from their European ancestors. The wool-covered leather shako with its shiny leather vizor, red plume and ornate badge was soon found to be impractical and was abandoned in favor of the kepi or "Hardee" hat.

Tunic: The dark blue shell jacket with its red adornments and high collar was soon withdrawn from service but nevertheless remained popular "informal" wear among many of the older soldiers.

Weapons: Defense was delegated to specially trained infantry units. Nevertheless, many gunners were issued with long, curved sabers which most soon abandoned as too heavy and impractical.

that, although the Army of the Potomac had only nine incomplete batteries with a total of 30 pieces when it was formed, by the time it was ready to take to the field, its artillery had been increased to 92 batteries with 520 pieces and a strength of 12,500 men. Years of experience had taught Barry that artillery was too important to be handled by half-trained amateurs. Accordingly, batteries of regular artillery were withdrawn from the outlying forts and coastal batteries (it having been correctly assessed that the Confederacy did not then have the strength to attack the latter) and transferred to the ranks of the Army of the Potomac as field gunners. By August 1861, over half of the regular gunners in the Union army were stationed under McClellan's command in the Washington area.

As the war progressed, it was realized that Barry's innovations, however good, did not utilize the dreadful potential of artillery to its full extent. After the Battle of Chancellorsville (1–6 May 1863), the four divisional batteries were removed, consolidated into artillery brigades, and allocated direct to the corps commander. Simultaneously, horse artillery, which had become unfashionable after the Mexican War, was returned to favor and attached in increasing numbers to the cavalry.

Field artillery was invariably positioned in the very front lines of the troops that it was supporting, with the result that losses to counter-battery artillery and snipers were inevitably high. During the Spotsylvania campaign (8–20 May 1864), Battery "C", 5th U.S. Artillery found itself in action ahead

of its own front line and immediately attracted enemy fire. The left-flank gun succeeded in discharging nine rounds before it was silenced; another managed 14 rounds. By the end of the action, 22 of the 24 gunners had been wounded, seven of them fatally. Every horse had been killed and the limbers rendered useless by enemy cannon and rifle fire. Such was the nature of close-quarter artillery engagement.

The organization and support provided to the artillery by the individual states within the Union varied tremendously. Regiments, battalions, and even independent batteries were raised on an *ad hoc* basis to fulfill Washington's insatiable desire for specialist units. Delaware produced one battery of light guns, while the far more affluent and secure states of Massachusetts and New York donated 17 and 36 independent batteries respectively. Once raised, individual units might expect to serve in a variety of capacities. Although most horse artillery units comprised regulars, due presumably to their known ability to ride, volunteer field gunners were occasionally seconded to the cavalry with mixed results. In times of greatest need, less fortunate gunners (presumably those who found themselves in the wrong place at the wrong time) were even "relegated" to the infantry.

In the early stages of the war, muzzle-loading, smoothbore cannon – some with ranges little in excess of those of rifle-muskets – dominated the battlefield, but as the conflict progressed, these were gradually replaced by a new generation of

Battery D, 5th U.S. Artillery deploy for action.

more powerful rifled weapons. Breechloaders were experimented with but remained unpopular with the conservatives in overall command in Washington.

The most common gun in service with both armies was the ubiquitous light 6-pounder, a simple smoothbore muzzle-loader mounted on a two-wheeled, wooden "stock trail" carriage pulled by a pair of horses. Less numerous but far more successful and popular was the "Napoleon," a bronze 12-pounder designed by Emperor Napoleon III and first used by the French in the Crimea. Lighter by 530 lb (240kg) and shorter by 12 inches (30cm) than the Model 1841 12-pounder which it replaced, it could nevertheless project a 12 lb (5.5kg) shot (identical to that fired by the Model 1841) 1,620 yards (1,480m), virtually as far as its much larger predecessor.

Local battery defense was delegated to specially trained infantrymen rather than to the gunners themselves who were not issued with muskets. Some, however, were issued with pistols, while others received large, sharply curved, brass-hilted sabers which were generally considered to be more of a hindrance than a help in close quarters.

In accord with the fashion of the day, light artillerymen wore distinctive uniforms which owed much to their European heritage. For dress, a tall, wool-covered leather shako topped, tailed, and vizored with shiny leather was issued. A single red worsted cord, decorated at either end with a tassel, ran from the left to right side of the shako to prevent the unwieldy headpiece falling off the wearer's head in rough conditions. It was secured to the tunic by a further red cord which passed down the back, under the arm and then attached to the third upper button. Two large, worsted, tassels of circular, interwoven design decorated the front of the cord. A brass crossed-cannon badge with the regimental number below and battery letter above the central point was worn beneath a brass eagle plate, the whole surmounted by a large plume of red horsehair.

A dark blue cloth shell jacket – decorated with a row of 12 small, equidistant buttons and a narrow strip of red lace along the front and around the entire lower edge – formed part of the dress uniform. Officers' shoulder straps, N.C.O.'s chevrons and trouser strips were also of red. Uniquely, the artillery was never issued with dark blue trousers, wearing from the outset the light blue pattern destined to become universal issue.

When hostilities commenced, the full dress uniform was almost immediately replaced by the standard fatigue dress, and it is doubtful if many volunteer units ever received the shakos and shell jackets. Although regular units were quick to replace the unwieldy shako with the more practical "Hardee" hat, the dress jackets, featuring the "Russian" shoulder knot with the silver insignia of rank in the case of the officers, remained popular and continued to be worn in the field by a number of units and individuals despite orders to the contrary.

Light artillery could only operate within range of enemy snipers. Casualties were therefore high and crews frequently supplemented by untrained infantrymen.

U.S. NAVAL OFFICER

At the outbreak of hostilities, the U.S. navy was in no fit state to undertake the blockade of the South demanded of it. Anticipating secession, John B. Floyd, the Secretary of War and a latent Confederate sympathizer, had sent five ships to the East Indies, three to Brazil, seven to the Pacific, three to the Mediterranean, and seven to the coast of Africa. In February 1861, only two steamships – the 25-gun *Brooklyn* and the *Relief* with two guns – remained in domestic waters, the latter under orders to sail with supplies for the Africa squadron. Twenty-eight ships languished in home ports, decommissioned and unfit for immediate service. Funds made available for maintenance and repairs had simply not been spent.

The already critical situation was made worse soon after the attack on Fort Sumter, when the defenders of Norfolk, Virginia overreacted to a Confederate attack and destroyed ten warships and most of the naval supplies rather than let them fall into enemy hands. To compound the problem, they failed in their attempt to destroy large numbers of cannon in storage in the Norfolk navy yard thus presenting the South with 3,000 pieces of ordnance with which to equip its own fledgling fleet.

Gideon Welles, Secretary of the Navy, and Gustavus Fox, his Assistant Secretary, tirelessly and efficiently set about the task of rebuilding the navy. Every seaport in the North was scoured and all suit-able ships bought, chartered, or commandeered. Orders were placed with government yards for eight new sloops while private tenders went out for the production of 23 screw gunboats. Shipbuilding continued unabated throughout the war until, by mid-1865, the Federal navy had swelled from its original 23 warships to a staggering 641 ships of all types.

So huge an increase in shipping inevitably led to manning problems. In 1861, the 1,457 officers and 7,600 men of the U.S. navy were demoralized, a situation made no better when 16 captains, 34 commanders, 76 lieutenants and 111 regular and active midshipmen defected to the Confederacy. Nevertheless, as the war progressed, the navy managed to produce officers of sufficient mental flexibility to handle the radically new ships and tactics then being adopted.

The problem was compounded considerably by the introduction in the 1860's of revolutionary new methods of propulsion and armored protection. The standard warships of the day were still of wooden construction with masts and sail providing the main means of propulsion. However, by now the steam engine had become a practical machine with the result that the latest ships were fitted with screws or paddles to provide an alternative method of movement. Although not totally reliable, steam power provided a degree of maneuverability

The Naval Practice Battery, Washington – in the background are a Dahlgren rifled gun and Cochran breech loader.

Badges of rank: After 1863 captains, as depicted here, wore three gold lace rings on each sleeve. Rank was also denoted on the shoulder boards.

Frock coat: Traditionally deck officers wore a dark blue frock coat with high collar and two rows of nine buttons each. Most officers wore the jacket undone to reveal the waistcoat worn underneath. Many abandoned the cumbersome coat completely in favor of more comfortable privately purchased civilian attire.

Weapons: Deck officers carried a Model 1852 sword ideally suited to close quarter fighting. Many also carried a variety of privately purchased knives and pistols.

previously undreamed of, and destined to prove of crucial importance in the river battles ahead.

More fundamentally, warships were taking on a completely new design. In 1858, the French began the construction of *La Gloire*, the world's first sea-going ironclad warship, and a year later the British responded with *Warrior*, not only ironclad but built entirely of iron. Earlier attempts by the French navy to operate floating batteries of heavy guns, protected by iron, had proved successful in the Crimean War, as a result of which many naval authorities, including the Confederates, began toying with the idea of mounting large guns on "unsinkable" platforms. Therefore, not only did the Union have to appoint a large number of new deck officers to swell its depleted ranks but it also had to create from nowhere naval traditions in long-range gunnery and engineering.

Perhaps because of its tendency to operate far from home, the pre-war navy had developed traditions of dress, discipline, and class very different to those of the army. Black sailors served below deck without let or hindrance and, after the outbreak of hostilities, were commissioned. The very best, such as Captain Robert Smalls of the gunship *Planter* actually attained command.

Prior to 1862, only the commissioned ranks of captain, commander, and lieutenant existed. However, to accommodate the rapid expansion of the navy during the war, the ranks of lieutenant commander, commodore, and admiral were reintroduced in 1862 and a new system of rank marking devised in 1863.

Throughout the war, the basic officer's uniform consisted of a dark blue, double-breasted frock coat. Individual appointments were denoted by the pattern of buttons: deck officers besported two rows of nine buttons each; until February 1861, engineers wore only a single row of buttons; secretaries wore a row of eight buttons and clerks six. All wore dark blue wool trousers in winter and white duck or linen in summer. Officers were permitted to wear double-breasted blue wool or white drill jackets when at sea, but with the exception of young graduates straight from the naval academy at Annapolis – for whom the dress presumably gave status – few actually did. The ornate dress uniform of tail coat and standing collar, cocked hat, gold-trimmed trousers and heavy gold epaulettes was abandoned early in the war as too expensive. As demand outstripped supply and the ranks became swelled by those who saw their sole task as the destruction of the enemy, standards of dress and tradition were often compromised in the name of expediency. Officers began to dress for comfort rather than sartorial elegance. "Sack coats," more familiar on the battlefield than at sea, began to replace the more formal and less practical frock coat. As is so often the case, officers who provided their own clothing at their own expense soon began to demand more personalized cuts and embellishments until, by 1862, few officers showed any real signs of uniformity.

Prior to the introduction of the new rank structure, captains wore three gold stripes around each cuff, commanders two, and lieutenants one. Masters wore three buttons parallel to the cuff and

midshipmen none, presumably relying upon the cut of their uniform to denote their somewhat dubious status. Dark blue shoulder straps edged in gold embroidery further denoted rank. A captain wore an eagle over an anchor, a commander two fouled anchors, a lieutenant a single fouled anchor, and a master plain straps with no insignia. A qualified midshipman wore a narrow gold strip on each shoulder. Similar insignia within a gold wreath were worn by the senior commissioned ranks as cap badges, masters and midshipmen wearing a fouled anchor on its side within a wreath. Engineers, pursers, surgeons, and other specialists each wore distinctive insignia denoting their rank and status.

When new ranks were introduced on 16 July 1862, confusion reigned supreme. Rear Admirals wore three wide and three narrow gold cuff stripes, a captain three wide stripes, a commander two wide and one narrow stripe, a lieutenant commander two wide stripes, and a lieutenant a single narrow stripe over a wide one. The full status of the ranks of master and midshipman were now recognized by the awarding of, respectively, a single wide and a single narrow stripe. Cap badges were simplified as were shoulder boards, which now took on a distinctly military air.

Badges of rank were altered yet again, this time fundamentally, in May 1863. All officers wore thin gold stripes on their sleeves to indicate seniority. Ensigns, the most junior rank, wore one stripe while rear admirals, the most senior, wore eight. Line officers were identifiable by a gold star worn centrally above the top stripe. Specialists, whose ostentatious insignia had made them easy prey for snipers, now adopted standard badges of rank save for their cap badges which continued to denote their arm of service.

Officers were armed with the Model 1852 sword with a fishskin grip and brass hilt featuring a design incorporating oak leaves, acorns, and the letters "USN." With its slightly curved blade, the sword was essentially similar to that carried by officers today. Despite the horrendous power of the ships' guns of the day, close-quarter, cross-deck fighting between crews remained a particularly savage aspect of combat. Officers, particularly those in charge of boarding parties or guns, therefore carried not only regulation pistols holstered on the right hip but also, on occasion, a variety of knives and axes including the highly effective Dahlgren knife-bayonet.

Officers of the U.S.S. *Monitor* pose for a photograph during a patrol of the James River.

Facing page: Sailors pose on the deck of the U.S.S. *New Hampshire*. The formal naval uniforms would have been relaxed at sea.

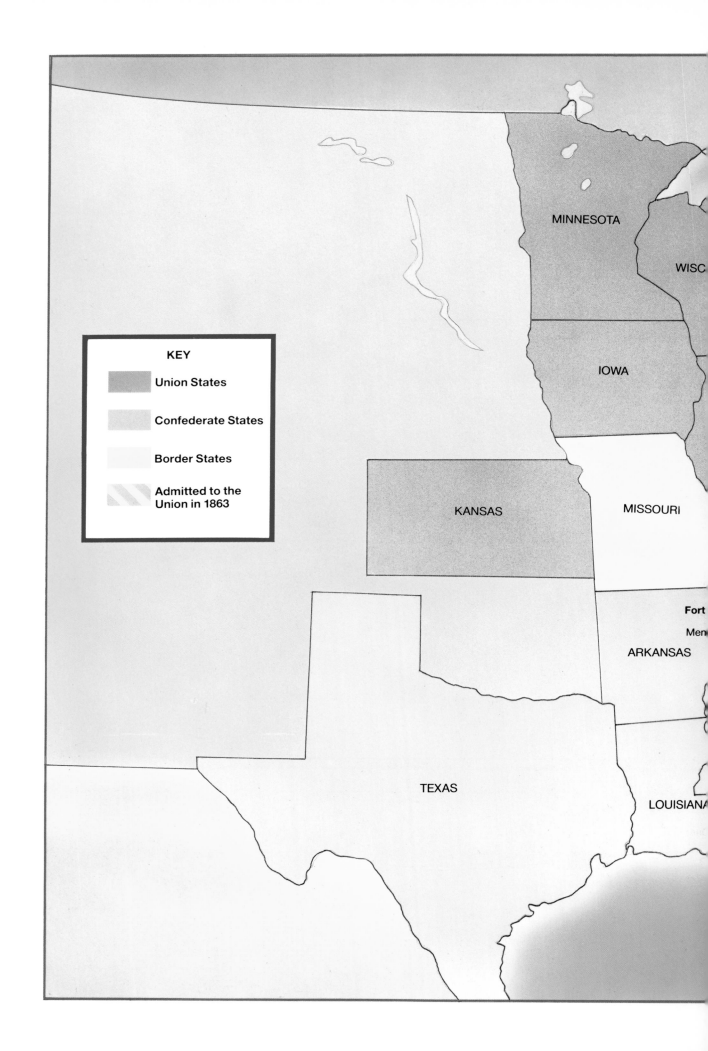

KEY

Union States

Confederate States

Border States

Admitted to the
Union in 1863

MINNESOTA

WISC

IOWA

KANSAS

MISSOURI

Fort

Men

ARKANSAS

TEXAS

LOUISIANA

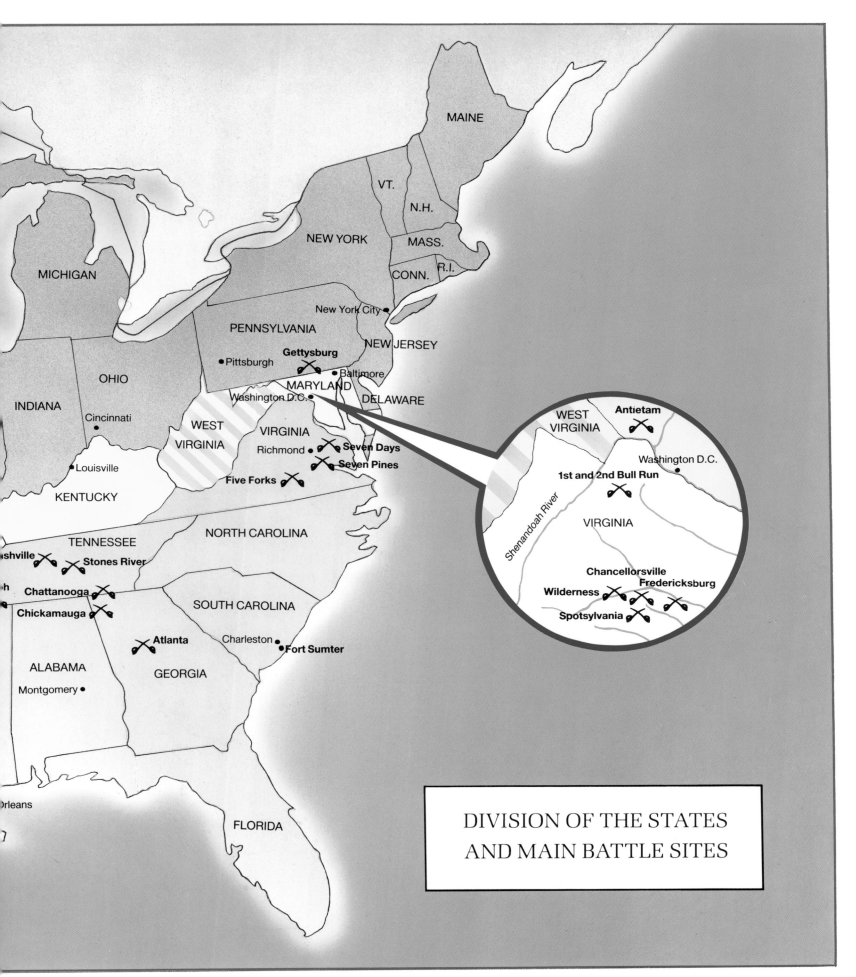

MAINE

VT.

N.H.

NEW YORK

MASS.

CONN.   R.I.

MICHIGAN

New York City •

PENNSYLVANIA

NEW JERSEY

• Pittsburgh   **Gettysburg**

OHIO

• Baltimore

MARYLAND

INDIANA

Washington D.C. •

DELAWARE

• Cincinnati

WEST
VIRGINIA

VIRGINIA

Richmond •   **Seven Days**

Seven Pines

• Louisville

Five Forks

KENTUCKY

NORTH CAROLINA

TENNESSEE

shville   **Stones River**

h

Chattanooga

SOUTH CAROLINA

Chickamauga

Atlanta

Charleston •

• **Fort Sumter**

ALABAMA

GEORGIA

Montgomery •

Orleans

FLORIDA

WEST
VIRGINIA   **Antietam**

Washington D.C. •

1st and 2nd Bull Run

Shenandoah River

VIRGINIA

Chancellorsville
Fredericksburg

Wilderness

Spotsylvania

DIVISION OF THE STATES
AND MAIN BATTLE SITES

57

BADGES OF RANK: U.S. ARMY

EPAULETTES

LIEUT. GENERAL

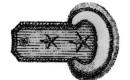

MAJOR GENERAL

BRIGADIER GENERAL

COLONEL

LIEUT. COLONEL

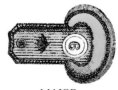

MAJOR

FIRST LIEUTENANT

CAPTAIN

SECOND LIEUTENANT

SHOULDER STRAPS

LIEUT. GENERAL

COLONEL

CAPTAIN

MAJOR GENERAL

LIEUT. COLONEL

FIRST LIEUTENANT

BRIGADIER GENERAL

MAJOR

SECOND LIEUTENANT

CHEVRONS

| SERGT. MAJOR | QUARTER-MASTER SERGT. | ORDNANCE SERGT. | HOSPITAL STEWARD | FIRST SERGT. | SERGEANT | CORPORAL | PIONEER |

Index

Acknowledgements
4 volume set (originally published as Combat
Uniforms of the Civil War)

Alabama Department of Archives and History,
Hulton Getty, Library of Congress, Museum of
the Confederacy, National Archives, North
Carolina State Division of Archives, Peter
Newark's Western Americana, Smithsonian
Institution, Texas State Library, Virginia
Military Institute.